ZODIAC

SURREY

Edited by Lucy Jeacock

First published in Great Britain in 2002 by
YOUNG WRITERS
Remus House,
Coltsfoot Drive,
Peterborough, PE2 9JX
Telephone (01733) 890066

HB ISBN 0 75433 626 3
SB ISBN 0 75433 627 1

FOREWORD

Young Writers was established in 1991 with the aim of promoting creative writing in children, to make reading and writing poetry fun.

Once again, this year proved to be a tremendous success with over 41,000 entries received nationwide.

The Zodiac competition has shown us the high standard of work and effort that children are capable of today. The competition has given us a vivid insight into the thoughts and experiences of today's younger generation. It is a reflection of the enthusiasm and creativity that teachers have injected into their pupils, and it shines clearly within this anthology.

The task of selecting poems was a difficult one, but nevertheless, an enjoyable experience. We hope you are as pleased with the final selection in *Zodiac Surrey* as we are.

CONTENTS

Emily Gemma Haynes	70
Alex Barron	71
Kimberley-Jayne Stoneman	71
Emily Skinner	72
Rachel Collum	73
Jessica Jones	74
Natasha Mitchell	74
Eleanor Rae	75
Natasha Bhana	76
Abigail Watson	77
Jenny Stevens	78
Verity Marie Lambert	79
Georgina Wilkins	80
Hannah Liddle	80
Katie Hamilton	81
Katie Holden	82
Misba Rashid	82
Francoise Trappey	83
Emma Burvill	84
Ruth Munroe	84
Kirina Wright	85
Sophie O'Connor	86
Eleanor Wells	86
Caroline Drew	87
Calandra Stone	88
Stephanie Gibson	89
Charlotte Main	90
Katie Jillings	91
Laura Clemson	92
Carlie Cheall	93
Lisa Kerr	94
Frances Andrews	95
Jennifer Ramsdale	96
Catherine Hyatt	97
Denali Meyers	98
Janhavi Rane	98
Chloe Tangney	99
Hattie Ellis	100

Andrea Bent	154
Deborah Pearse	154
Lucy Moon	155
Stuart Burrows	156
Francesca Hoyle	157
Monique Davis	158
Daniella McCarthy	159
Matthew Hurst	159
Martin Matthews	160
Kayleigh-Jade Telfer	160
Samantha Harding	161
Ben Makroum	162
Charlotte Webb	162
Brianne Marsden	163
Iain Powell	163
Rickey Bourne	164

Whitgift School

Luke Dickerson	164
Ross Netherway	165
Martin Brown	166
Ion Martea	166
Savio Moniz	167
Alex Dawson	168
Ben Winstanley	169
Sebastian Wood	170
Daniel Lou	170
James Daly	171
Duncan Watson-Steward	172
Edward Ash	173
Ben McFadden	174
Tom Bond	175
Alex Forbes	176
Andrew McGrath	177
Adil Malik	178
Charlie Tuckey	179
Anuj Mohindra	180
William Hall	181

The Poems

LOVE IS LIKE

What is love . . .

Love is like a maze
You can easily get lost
Your heart's set ablaze
At such a big cost
You approach it from every angle
As soon as your heart sings
You know you've found your angel
You know what love can bring

Love is like a runaway train
You go along for the ride
It can give and take the pain
It can also leave you behind
Don't miss your last journey
From way up above
This beautiful thing in front of me
Just happens to be love
Love is like what I've found
It's really nice to be around.

Amy Burger (15)

TO THE MILLENNIUM

I saw the last 12 years of you, and heard of the other 88,
You taught me all that I know of people, of history,
and of human limits,
You laid before me legacies of war and peace, of human compassion
and cruelty, and of conflict and resolution.
And yet you present me with chances without limits,
to change our future.

Mardean Isaac (12)

WHAT IF . . .

What if the sky was merry and red,
The grass was a dark purple though you were too,
What if the school finished early instead of late.
What if the old bell chimed like dingle goo,
The teachers were huge bloodthirsty monsters,
What about you?
Scales of thick plates of bulletproof armour!
What if the school was a bully's prison camp,
The cars are mega devastating demolition tanks.
What if the classes were sphere-like and gold,
This place would be a nightmare!
All this would never be true.
Almost . . .

Oliver Davies (13)

THE BEAUTIFUL STARS

The stars, the stars, what a beautiful sight,
The stars, the stars, shimmer all night.
The stars are bright and reflect the light,
The stars, the stars, what a beautiful sight.

If one night you're feeling down, look up to the stars,
You wish that you could be somewhere else,
like far away in Mars.

The boldest and brightest star you must find,
Make a wish and leave your troubles behind.

The stars, the stars, a golden white,
The stars, the stars, what a beautiful sight.

Kelly Stokes (13)
Bishopsford Community School

LIFE AT WAR

Marching towards the flashes
Seeing the flare lights
Curving over the trenches
The noise
Bang, bang, louder and louder
Shells casing over
Whoo-oo-ooooo, *ooo, bump, crash!*
Flop! Flop! Little pieces of shell casing

People in trenches eating
Bread, bacon, rum and bitter tea
Hundreds of field mice and frogs crawling
Squeak, squeak
Ribbet, ribbet
Wet and slippery trenches
Squelch, squelch
Cigarettes, guns and bullets
All over the place
Bandages, blood
On floors

Gas alarms
Whoo-whoo-whooo
Gas a killing machine
Which blinds and burns inside
Within 45 minutes everyone dies
They send us across no-man's-land
Where we find out
What this war is really about
Many friends have died
Few have survived
War is not what you think it is.

Shakeel Ahmad Bhatti (13)
Bishopsford Community School

STARS IN THEIR EYES

There it lies
The stars in their eyes
The more their imaginations
The fainter the stars appear
The more they walk
The lesser their brain is
Maybe that is their luck
There it lies
The stars in their eyes
In the eyes of the bull
And the exposure in the eyes of a scorpion
Taurus or Scorpio, a prolonged exposure
Minute by minute
More and more of the dim, luminosity
Shed by a globular cluster in Hercules
Achieving a feat far beyond
The capability of the human eye
From east to north
South to west
360 degrees is nothing in their eyes
Neither are the minutes
But nothing changes in their life
Till they turn and smile
Life is full of surprises.

Angel Ajidahun (13)
Bishopsford Community School

4

THE BIG DAY!

I remember the first day I signed up,
I couldn't believe my luck,
I packed up my bags,
And put in some fags.
When I got there then,
There were thousands of men.

There were trenches,
Which had no benches.
We were told to attack,
Some of us never came back.
One of my friends was lying there,
Wishing that they weren't dying here.

Lots of people had diseases,
Which made them keep on sneezing.
They ate our bully beef, the rats,
Which made them very, very fat.
I'm glad I got home safe,
But I don't feel the same,
I miss my friends so much,
War wasn't much fun,
I remember the first day I signed up.

Kylie Botchway (13)
Bishopsford Community School

A DAY NEVER TO BE FORGOTTEN
(In memory of all the people that were killed on that day)

We sat and watched in disbelief,
At thousands of people full of grief.
I think of all the people across the Atlantic,
That must have been running around very frantic.
Something happened we'd always remember,
Never forget the 11th of September.

People died in the hands of madman,
A maniac called Osama bin Laden.
Although it's sad and there is no joy, just think of
every little girl and boy,
Who lost their parents on that day.
And so we bow our heads and pray,
For those lives lost upon that day.
I will never forget the tragedy I saw,
Which now means we're at war!

Debbie Johnson (13)
Bishopsford Community School

STARGAZER

Stargazer, gazer midnight raiser,
as I wake, you call stargazer.
Midnight tool there's a call for you star night tool.
In the sky there's a mix of colours
a midnight fix all for others.
There's a touch of magic, an ounce of pure delight,
I could stay here every night.
Stargazer, gazer midnight raiser,
as I wake, you sing *stargazer.*

Robert J Sykes (13)
Bishopsford Community School

THINGS I THINK ABOUT WHEN I SAY 'LOVE'

Love is a dress
In its own fashion
When you are dressed in it
Everybody wants to wear it

Love is a book
That has never been written
Be the first to write it
And the world will read it

Love is food
That's very nourishing
Cook it
And be nourished by it

Love is shelter
A shelter for me and you
Let's be sheltered by it
Away from the cold and heat

Love is education
No professor has taught it
Study love
And be a professor of love

Love doesn't divide, it multiplies
Love doesn't hate other, it loves other
Love doesn't destroy, it builds
Try to be swimming in love
And you will enjoy the rest of your days.

Juliet Beah (13)
Bishopsford Community School

MY MUM

She's caring and affectionate and sometimes rather barmy
I think she is quite clever and always says things rather calmly
She can be very dangerous if she's in a mood
She can be really embarrassing and sometimes very rude
She is a rather little woman but she's very cool
I think I forgot to mention, she works in a school
She doesn't like it when it starts to rain
Support is what she gives me, courage is what I gain
If I'm sad she makes me a cup of tea
And she always seems to understand, always seems to see
Christmas is the best time of the year
It is never glum
She always is very happy and acts like she is young
But when she's old I'll take her to the zoo
Because she is my mum.

David Crump (12)
Bishopsford Community School

SPACE

The final frontier!
We are so close but yet so far
We look up every night
and see a new star shining bright in the night sky
As planets turn and galaxies are formed
we look endlessly at the dark area we call space
We know more about the moon than we do about Mars
Who knows, there might be life out there
on other planets and galaxies that thrive.

Nathan Miller (13)
Bishopsford Community School

MY DREAM POEM

She has her own special fragrance
And rosy red cheeks.
She is rather unique,
Caring and kind.
She is like a zebra wearing black and white,
Helpful and nice.
She is outgoing, youthful and full of life,
Generous and joyful.
She is boisterous, but patient
And will always sympathise.
She is imaginative and has vibe.
She is quick on her feet,
Dark and tall.
She is mysterious and wishful
That I'll have a great life!

That is my *mum!*

Rosie Pyett (12)
Bishopsford Community School

ALIENS

Past the sun is the land of people,
Glow do the heavens past many moons,
Power up the shield through the wormhole,
Stop . . . asteroid field, comets, space,
Eclipse on impact with 'life-likes'!
Aliens, aliens, starry blue and green,
Black hole to left, meteor belt to right,
Contact? Strange little beings,
Call themselves Ôomans!

Kerry Costelloe (13)
Bishopsford Community School

ZODIAC

It's amazing to me,
What you can see,
When you look into the sky,
And see the stars fly,
Like an accelerating dart,
And this is just the start.
There are millions out there,
This makes me stare,
Into the sky,
As more stars fly.
There are star signs too,
For different months all year through.
Mine is Virgo,
There are others, like Scorpio,
They are supposed to be about you,
But for me that's not true.
It's amazing to me,
What you can see,
When you look into the sky,
And see the stars fly.

James Crook (13)
Bishopsford Community School

ZODIAC

Stars, planets, the sky
Black with white dots in a clear sky
Scorpion, lion, Aquarius
Mercury, Venus, Earth, Mars, Jupiter, Saturn, Uranus, Neptune, Pluto
Everything up in the sky like stars
Satellites, comets, Milky Way
All part of what we call zodiac

Stars, planets, the sky
Black with white dots on a clear sky
Black holes acting like whirlpools
Sucking in gas and stars
Planets, stars and the Milky Way
All part of what we call the zodiac.

Michael Bourke (12)
Bishopsford Community School

AN INTERGALACTIC WAR

Balls of fire
Whizzing past at the speed of light
Causing minor dents
In the thick, metal of the war shuttle
'Damage report!' cries the captain
'Shields down,' says the computer
And as the captain curses
The pilot's wing explodes
And into the nothingness of space
Drifts the enemy shuttle's rubble

But the war is barely over
As hundreds more appear
And finally the enemy's base explodes
The good guys start to cheer
The rubble drifts into the sun
The hundreds depleted into one
And it was then destroyed
And the good guys throw a party
For they had won the war.

James Dawes (13)
Bishopsford Community School

A SPACE POEM

The sign's to tell you what will happen
In the month that things will happen
There in the darkness of the sky
Up so very high in that dark blue sky
Are stars that make up your sign

In space the planets spin round and round
The moon is there all yellow and sometimes round
A full moon, half moon and sometimes a total eclipse
My star sign is Cancer the crab and so is my nan's
As our birthdays are in July

It would be fun in space
There would be no gravity and we would be floating everywhere
But I really wouldn't care
Unless I got sucked into a black hole in space
And time would travel as if I was in a race
I'm glad I'm on the ground again
Where I am safe until the next time
I think about space.

Ashley Chaplin (12)
Bishopsford Community School

MARS

M is for meteorites that fly up in space
A is for astronauts that go into space
R is for rockets that fly to space
S is for stars up in space.

Sarah Balaam (12)
Bishopsford Community School

SWEET DREAMS

Her eyes are like precious jewels
that gleam and sparkle in the light.
She is extremely intelligent and ever so kind.
She has a wonderful, bright personality
and she's talented in so many ways.
Her youth is everlasting and she moves with such elegance.
She's outgoing and adventurous and at the same time she's friendly.
She glides heavenly looking as lovely as usual.
She likes to keep things neat and tidy,
being cheerful and not too harsh.
In her spare time she likes to relax
and expects to get treated like a queen.
She's unbelievable and zealous
and when she talks the words glide through my mind.
Her way of doing things is vibrant and enthusiastic.
The person I'm talking about is my mum.

Chanel Daley (12)
Bishopsford Community School

BLACK HOLE

B   urning up all space
L   ike a flame thrower
A   lways looking for more
C   losing its deadly jaws
K   eeping ships forever in the pit of despair

H   olding ships with its tongues
O   pening its mouth till it's too . . .
L   ate . . . it's gone
E   verlasting turmoil enclosing on all.

Heather Smith (14)
Bishopsford Community School

IS THERE FATE?

One day I went for a walk in the park,
I waved hello to a boy called Mark.
I walked and walked until I couldn't anymore,
Then I tripped up and fell on the floor.
But then to my surprise,
I slipped on a couple of fries.
A boy helped me up,
But I was stuck,
My bum was stuck to a load of muck.
He pulled and pulled,
Until he falled.
We were both lying on the floor,
And we were both sure,
We had found a mate,
There is a fate.

Debbie Showell (13)
Bishopsford Community School

STARS ARE FRIENDS

Stars are bright
Stars are small
Stars are cool
Stars are little
Stars are tall
Stars rule
Stars are friends
Stars are mates
Stars are best.

Steven Shearman (12)
Bishopsford Community School

MY FAMILY OF STARS

Taurus standing tall,
Never to be beaten.

Taurus standing proud,
Never to back down.
Taurus, my star sign,
I will live up to thee.

Leo, the faithful one,
Will stand by you.
Leo, the loving one,
In times of difficulty.
Leo, my sister's star sign,
She will live up to thee.

Capricorn, always practical,
Takes time and care.
Capricorn, always patient,
Making list upon list.
Capricorn, my dad's star sign,
He will live up to thee (hopefully!)

Pisces, the sensitive person,
Always ready to talk.
Pisces, the kind and caring person,
Always understands.
Pisces, my mum's star sign,
She will live up to thee.

Carl Whittaker (13)
Bishopsford Community School

POEM

I look up at the black sheet above me,
I wonder what creatures live up there and what will I see,
I see stars everywhere, shining bright,
I see lots of different shapes, lots of lights.
I'm all alone on this adventure, searching for something up there!

I imagine myself in a spaceship searching for life,
All alone, no family, no friends, no wife,
Nobody cared about me on Earth,
Nobody wanted me, even at my birth,
So, I'm going away and never coming back,
Searching for something, anything, until
Crash!

I'm going down fast, losing control,
I'll never survive this, but no one will know.
If I made this discovery, I'd be popular for sure.
Everyone would want to know and they'd want more,
So, I shut my eyes and prayed,
Guess what, *they* saved my day!
I was taken to their planet, far, far away,
I was living there yesterday and still am today!

Rachel Vickers (12)
Bishopsford Community School

THE MOON WE SEE ON EARTH

Billions of years old,
a place in space,
a place with so much dust,
that with one step it goes in your face.
I wonder what the dinosaurs thought
of this bright thing in the sky?
They probably thought it was the trillion year old sun
just about to die.

The moon must get dizzy,
spinning round and round.
It has no one to talk to,
it has never heard a sound.
Its friends are all in different planets,
burning or freezing to death.
It never chose to be a moon
and will never choose again.

Naima Khalid (13)
Bishopsford Community School

STAR SIGNS

Aquarius

You can look through the
future with your eyes
time won't pass by.
Just trust in yourself
and do what you can.

Pisces

You can always be sensitive,
just try to be loud.
Maybe, just
maybe you might
get something
out of it.

Taurus

A strong bull.
So mighty in the sky.
Always looking above
day and night.

Stella Naluwooza (13)
Bishopsford Community School

FIDGET!

My cat is the loveliest cat in the world
He is black and white and I love him
I have another called Misty, but she is my sister's cat.

Fidget sleeps in my bed every night
And when I wake up in the morning he is still lying there
He follows me everywhere
He even follows me to the bus stop in the morning
And then goes back home when I get on the bus.

I feed him all the time and bath him once a week
He actually likes getting wet.

He is one year and three months and he still has growing to do
He is a small cat and very energetic
He catches mice and frogs and all sorts of insects
And brings them in to me and drops them at my feet.

So that is my cat and I love him very much.

Cassie Edwards (12)
Bishopsford Community School

SPACE

Space is like an ocean
Space is like the sea
What a wonderful place to be
To walk in history

Some people say to fly away is
The best thing in the world
But other people think to sink into the ink
Of space is the worst thing in the world

One day I was walking by
When I caught a guy up in the Millennium Eye
Trying to fly to the moon in the sky
But fell and died by the Millennium Eye.

Ryan Burge (12)
Bishopsford Community School

BRO

Like an *ape* he flies around the room
And sometimes he hits the TV and it goes *boom*
He a bodily guy
And if he hits you, you will fly
He loves his *candy*
Not like he loves his girlfriend Mandy
He is a *dribbler* that's what he is
No, no, no, I think it is his *eagerness*

Falling over, grazing his knees
And falling over and breaking his keys
He is such a *hazard* sort of guy
And he is an ignoramus
Jabbering, jabbering all day long
Knackered like a toy
He loves everything from TV and Anne Frank
Mental, noiseless and a bit odd as well as philanthropic
He's quick, rare and very silly as well
Sometimes he is a thief
Understanding, very wary
Xerox, yielding and zippy!

Billy Landymore (13)
Bishopsford Community School

FOOTBALL POEM

I really admire him
He is the best
Sometimes he is quite cocky
He is a brilliant dribbler
He was very expensive
He is fantastic
He can score a goal
Sometimes he can score a hat-trick
He was a big improvement
It was that he joined 'The Devils'
He is a killer to the defence
He is a leading player
He was a lot of money
His name is Ruud Van Nistelrooy
He is an offensive player
He came from PSV
He is very quick
He's very rampant
He is such a good striker
He is deadly in front of the goal
He might be unidentified
He's going on vacation
He needs an x-ray
Every year
He is wicked
He can zoom past the defence.

Tom Rowland (12)
Bishopsford Community School

MY MUM

My mum is an adventurous woman
She thinks she's really beautiful.
My mum is really cuddly
But she's really delicate.
My mum is really elegant
And normally always funny.
Mums are very important
And should always be joyful.
My mum is very kind
And always loud.
My mum is my mum
And she is very nice.
My mum is very optimistic
But usually very easy to please.
My mum is a very quick thinker
And always has to be right.
My mum's name is Sheryl
And she makes sure everything is tidy.
My mum is very unique
And quite vast.
My mum is very wild
And very xenophobic.
My mum is like a yo-yo
And is zippy.

Kirsty Smith (12)
Bishopsford Community School

ZODIAC

Flying to the next dimension
Into carriage, first so slow
Then so high and so, so fast
Going vertical
You feel as light as light
But as heavy as can be
Everything is blurred
Everything except me
Feeling like you're in space
All the stars and comets
The time continuum is just so slow
Time has stopped for me
And now it's coming back.

Cos I've just been for
A ride on the
Zodiac!

Stephen Brewster (13)
Bishopsford Community School

ZODIAC

In the sky so bright,
Everything happens at night,
But in the day the stars are away,
And the sun is shining light.

When the clouds come over,
And the rain starts to fall,
The lightning appears,
And strikes the ground with fire ball.

When the moon comes out,
And the stars twinkle bright,
Comets fly past
And zoom through the night.

When rockets go up,
And aliens say 'Hi!'
The moon lights up
And comes alive.

Stevie Blount (13)
Bishopsford Community School

ZODIAC

There are nine planets
In the universe
Which constantly reverse
And reverse
Earth, Saturn, Pluto, Mars
Those are all the well-known stars
When you look up to the sky
You see the stars shine up
So high
The moon is one of the stars
Which are strong
It changes its shape from
Short to long
There are nine planets
In the universe
And it's the end of this verse.

Alev Akar (13)
Bishopsford Community School

POEM

Space is a good place
Where you can stay
You can see stars
And also Mars
The sun is so bright
It's a wonderful sight

If you write
You feel so light
The moon reminds me of a balloon
Floating up to the sky
In space I could float
And you need a coat
I see shooting stars
While I'm on Mars.

Kenan Siqani (12)
Bishopsford Community School

SPACE

I flew to the moon
And I saw some stars
I dodged a black hole
And then landed on Mars.

I couldn't see any life
Not even a trace
This was the end of my journey
My journey in *space.*

Keri Trimmer (13)
Bishopsford Community School

BABOON POEM

He's my favourite character in my dream,
He glows in a very bright green!

He comes from a far away planet
And he makes a great pet.

His name is Bobo-Schmobo,
He just prefers to be called Bobo.

Bobo's favourite food is parsnip
With a little bit of barbecue dip.

And finally, sorry for keeping you waiting . . .
But it's time for Bobo's nappy changing!

Farhaz Mussa (13
Bishopsford Community School

SPACE

The Americans had a race
Neil Armstrong floating on the moon with grace
While the earth down below watched this TV show
Eclipses happen, but not for long
One happened in 1999 and now is gone
The star signs are supposed to be true
I don't believe in them, do you?
The planets and their moons revolve round, one by one
Aligning sometimes with the sun
It's not very often you see a comet
Now let's go in our rocket.

Andrew Harding (13)
Bishopsford Community School

MY MUM

My mum is an amazing person
She is a loveable, very cuddly person
My mum is a pretty person
She is a ravishing kind of person
In fact, she is the no 1 mum
My mum is the best mum in the world.

My mum doesn't like being ignored
She says that it is rude to ignore someone
My mum is like a yo-yo,
She is always going up and down to work
She is neat and tidy and is very finicky with the housework
Sometimes my mum gets depressed
But most of the time she is a merry, jolly, happy, witty
And glamorous person
I think my mum's hobby is to knit
Because she it very fast at it
My mum is a xenophobic, and brilliant person.
She is always energetic to get things done
My mum is a very special person in my life
And I hope we can never be apart.

Stacey Johnson (12)
Bishopsford Community School

SHE'S AMAZING

She is very amazing and beautiful
And also perfect.
She is knowledgeable and also educating,
She's perfect.
She's sensitive and radiant.
But sometimes she is nervous.
Joyful is what she is and definitely a queen.

Although she can be quite mysterious
And also she is a devil at times.
Caring is her middle name, and also helpful.
She's tremendously organised
And she is absolutely fantastic.

Tom Varney (12)
Bishopsford Community School

MY MUM, NO 1

Funny and generous, the best in the world,
always there, ready to help.
Decaffeinated coffee is what she drinks.
She's a very good listener, she's one of a kind.
She can't bear ironing, which she does *not* enjoy
but she always does it because she cares for us all.
She has a gold necklace, which says 'Mum',
I gave it to her one birthday.
She wears her perfume which makes her smell nice,
it smells like flowers, not too faint, but not too strong.
She is always open and ready to explain anything I want to know.
My mum is so understanding even when I am being silly.
She works in a school every day of the week
and every holiday she spends with me.
I admire my mum and respect her too.
She is as valuable to me as a really expensive diamond ring.
My mum is very tall and full of zeal and joy.
She is wonderful and I love her very much.

Emma Bone (12)
Bishopsford Community School

MY DREAM POEM

She's excellent, she's ace, she can't get any better
She's beautiful, she can light up a room with her graceful smile
She's great, no one can beat her
She makes the world a better place by existing
She's funny, she's like a good friend, always there, never an enemy
My mum is intelligent and mature
She is unique in her very own wonderful way
To me she's a queen and should be worshipped by people
She can really make a difference to people and my life
She is young and has a face and a voice of an angel
She has a certain zest about her
She is always trying to make my life better
And has done an excellent job
I love you Mum, you are great
And I know that we will be friends forever
I love you with all my heart and soul and my feelings will never change
My mum's name is Caroline, she also has a name like an angel.

Jade Howard (12)
Bishopsford Community School

SPACE

The land of space is a magnificent place,
Gravitation's tight and you fly like a kite.
Miles and miles up in the air,
Heading towards what they call the Great Bear.
Comets and shooting stars all array,
Glisten by night but never by day.

Matthew Burch (12)
Bishopsford Community School

MY MUM

My mum is very fun, she always looks beautiful
My mum loves perfume and sticks it on every day
Ever since she was twelve years old
She could draw anything, it was always perfect
My mum does a lot of walking
And when she is in a good mood she is full of happiness.

My mum will always be there for me and she is very kind
Whenever I have nothing to do
She always gives me something interesting to do.

My mother also loves nature, she hates seeing cruelty to animals
My mum likes to drink tea, day in and out
My mum always surprises you with something
And she is so wonderful.

Shalane Durrant (12)
Bishopsford Community School

DREAM POEM

Amazing is my mum's middle name
Her voice is like an operatic mogul
And still so daring and caring is she
She is so beautiful and radiant
As she walks down the street
Elaborate, loving but also stubborn she can be
She is so friendly and very happy too.
She is so very grateful for everything that I do
She's interesting and judicious and so very kind
Sometimes she is quiet but she can also be very nutty
She is a treasure, she is my mum.

Jacob Burge (12)
Bishopsford Community School

MY RABBIT FLOPSY

He is like a moon
Beaming in the sunlight
As precious and pretty as gold
Tranquil and angelic to heal the world.

It's as though he's a blanket
Wrapping me with love
My love for him will never depart.

He is unique, just like a star
Shining brightly no matter how far.

He is dynamic and valiant too
He is my rabbit Flopsy, so special, so cute.

He's soft and fluffy like a cloud
He always makes me so proud
No matter how old he gets
I'll always love him and never forget.

Karen Hitt (13)
Bishopsford Community School

MY MAD MUM IS NUMBER 1

She walks across me like a floating angel
She is the most brilliant mum, she's number 1
Cuddly and warm
Bright like daisies
Fun like a funfair
Her hair is so fair, silky and smooth
She's an individual, lovely and likable
Lovely and lazy, nutty and crazy

Kind and caring
Lovely and sharing
Scary and daring
Mad and annoying
Over active, silly and talkative
Perfect and great
There's only one word for my wonderful mum
It's *unbeatable!*

Kelly Harding (12)
Bishopsford Community School

THE SUN

I gaze into the sky,
Wondering if it will ever die.
At the crack of dawn it rises,
At dark it slowly sets to sleep.
The great ball of fire shines continuously,
Showing off its beautiful sight.
It is like a huge rope tied in a knot.

Safa Mohamed (12)
Bishopsford Community School

SPACE

Space consists of planets and stars
Jupiter, Saturn, Uranus and Mars.
Some have moons and some have rings,
Some have lots of very strange things.
Earth orbits the sun on its axis and sphere,
That's what makes a complete year.

Charlene Edwards (12)
Bishopsford Community School

MY CATS

My cats are probably the most adorable animals I have ever seen,
They are so blithe, so laid back, I wish I was them,
But occasionally they are most cheeky,
Though I still forgive them, as they are delicate,
They are full of energy and run everywhere,
But it is scary because they are so fragile,
They are gifted by being so soft,
But also they are frail,
Immature is not the word as they are so grown-up,
But they are sometimes jaunty.
I will always cherish the day I got my kittens,
Lazy is a word which describes them,
But monstrous is more like it,
As at nightfall they go out all night,
Their objection, catch a mouse and kill a mouse,
They work as a pair, side by side,
And as quick as anything they catch a mouse and kill a mouse,
Then at daybreak they reappear,
With satisfaction on their dark, little faces,
Not knowing how thoughtless they have been by taking a life,
They sense I am upset with their presence as they come up to me,
Rubbing their soft, velvet fur
I feel the warmth from their fur,
It's like being in bed waiting for Xmas,
Then they yawn, without a doubt they're tired, they get on their pillow
And close their eyes and dream of something zany.

Zoe Steptoe (12)
Bishopsford Community School

DREAM

She's always there for me, she's different from the rest
Caring is just one of her specialities
No matter if I'm away from her fabulous self
I have one thing to look forward to, I'll be seeing her soon
She's a role model in my life, so what if she's my opposite
Helpful, intelligent, kind and lively are just the things
I want from her and I needn't complain
At night when I close my eyes I see an extraordinary sight!

Someone with all the qualities, someone with brown hair
Someone with the attitude, someone musical, someone sweet
Someone truthful and someone vigorous
The sight continues more mysterious
I see golden light from all directions
I must admit, it's a wicked sight
I see a face emerging from the light
Shimmering, glittering stars surrounding a body
Like a million fairies surrounding a princess from a fairy tale itself
I am stunned, for a moment I forget to breath . . .
Ah, ah, ah, ah
And now I see the whole of the stunning personality
Beautiful brown eyes, a beautiful smile
Spread over the beautiful face . . .
And now I realise it' s none other than
My *'Mom'!*

Rida Tariq (12)
Bishopsford Community School

STARS

Stars shining down at night
Taurus running here and there during the starlight
A baby being born at that time
Really are there creatures in space?
Saturn spinning extravagantly

The stars up high in the sky
Shining down through the light
Moving slowly up and down
All the stars are up high
Go and visit them sometime
And that's the end of my journey.
    Goodbye!

Skye Seery (12)
Bishopsford Community School

THE PLANET OF THEM ALL

Milky Way,
Stars,
Galaxy and planets are all involved in
Space
The moon, the sun, Pluto
And Mars all sit in the sky
Gravity is floating
The Earth is a ball
So visit
Space and it will be the
Most fun of all.

Kayleigh Brock (12)
Bishopsford Community School

THE SPACE STATION

Floating in space
A tin can for people
The alarm bell rings
Red alert
An alien spacecraft sighted
Powerless to stop it
The alien boards
Tall and white with two black eyes
Then you realise you were dreaming
But now you're awake . . .
The invasion is real!

Jason Jacques (14)
Bishopsford Community School

STAGE STAR

He stands on stage playing on his Gibson
With blistering speed and wild sustain
His distortion takes over your brain
His heavy playing is like lightning
His unique quickness is calming the faster he goes
The magnificent vigorous and insightful overdrive
Makes the hairs on your back stand on end and your guts tighten
As he plays, the strings get rusty and his fingers bleed
The joyous but colossal playing is mad
His zippy, noisy playing matches with his yapping lyrics
The xylophone on his guitar was impressive
That's why I admire him.

John Lovell (12)
Bishopsford Community School

POEMZ

In the dark sky at night
All the stars shine so bright
The moon it has an eerie glow
That lights up the Earth below

Daylight brings the dawn sunlight
The sun it shines so warm and bright
At sunset time the sky grows red
And gives way to the moon in time for bed.

Lewis Barwise (12)
Bishopsford Community School

STEREO-SLAPPER

I'll be your belly dancer
I'll be your butterfly
I'll be your gypsy woman
I'll be your all-time high.

Stereo-slapper? And still a virgin . . . how?
Stereo-slapper. I still think I'm a wow!
Time goes by so fast
Memories forgotten along with the past
Just goes to show nothing good ever lasts.

I'll be your belly dancer
I'll be your butterfly
I'll be your gypsy woman
I'll be your all-time high.

Jean Graham (15)
Brit Performing Arts & Technology School

HE

He is the one, the one I think I love,
Sometimes I wonder if he was sent from above.
He knows I adore him, he knows how I feel,
Because my love is so strong it's hard to conceal.
I wish he would feel the same about me,
Because he is so perfect, with what I can see.
He has talent, enthusiasm, brains and wit,
He must have a fault but I can't seem to find it.
I think about him every day and sometimes at night,
I feel pain inside me when he is out of sight.
I'm holding onto something that isn't really there,
He doesn't want me, it's just so unfair.
I imagine us together, sharing thoughts and feelings,
He tells me he loves me, and other heart-warming things.
I can daydream for ages just looking at his face,
Then, *snap,* back to reality; I'm put in my place.
He's warm and friendly and has a good sense of style,
I could list all his good points, but it would take me a while.
It should be me and him, not him and her,
It will always be the opposite of what I prefer.
Will I love him forever? On this it will depend,
He'll probably do something to upset me, and that will be the end.
But for now he's still strong in my heart,
And he's still on my mind when we're apart.
When it's raining and he smiles at me, it brightens up my day,
I love him so much, more than words could ever say.

Catriona Jessie Lowe (15)
Brit Performing Arts & Technology School

LOVE IS

Love is such a powerful force
It can create and yet destroy
Mother love will last forever
Love makes the hardest man coy
Love and lust are mistaken as each other
Unreturned love is fatal
That's when you love someone and they don't love you
And there's nothing you can do
'Cause it sneaks upon you as if like sleep
And can hurt so bad
You almost weep
Some people retaliate against love
They're bitter, say there's no such thing
But I know and so do they
It lives in everything.

Jennifer Green (15)
Brit Performing Arts & Technology School

YOU COULD HAVE LIVED TOMORROW

Life is short until you've lived,
For death can be gone tomorrow.
Lived in years remembered in seconds,
It can all be erased tomorrow.
You've never lived but have always been living,
You could have lived tomorrow.

Benjamin Joel Robinson (16)
Coulsdon College

A WHOLE NIGHT'S WORK

As I scan the roof I ponder
My eyes are filled with awe and wonder
As they settle on my goal
For which I'd give my very soul.

My fingers work so deft and quick
Long wires, short wires, thick
I climb in so soft and light
Still gripping my Bo staff tight.

I search and search and find my prize
And it is so very small in size
A tiny diamond so bright and clear
Dancing like crystal or a tear.

Like an acrobat I jump and leap
Quietly I crawl and sneak and creep
Under laser beams and tripping wires
Like walking in Hell hot fires.

A few quick moves and I am out
Free again to stroll about
My prize is safely tucked away
Hidden from the very light of day.

Karen Louise Strugnell (16)
Coulsdon College

WINNIE THE POOH

If you were a character
In Winnie the Pooh
You wouldn't be Eeyore
'Cos he's too blue
You wouldn't be Piglet
'Cos he's too scared
You wouldn't be Tigger
He's unprepared
You would be that silly old bear
'Cos he has friendship he loves to share
Like Christopher Robin
And Winnie the Pooh
They are best friends
Like me and you.

Debbie Anderson (15)
Coulsdon High School

JUST ME

I'm fat, I'm thin
Big ears, flat feet
Big nose, small mouth
I'm shy, I'm loud
I'm short, I'm tall
I'm bad, I'm mad
I'm happy, I'm sad
I'm fast, I'm slow
Which way to go?
Just be yourself
Be kind and true
And people will look up to you.

Marina Nicoli (12)
Coulsdon High School

I WILL NEVER FORGET YOU

Every night in my dreams,
You're there, I see you.
A once in a lifetime feeling,
Embraced in the warmth of love.

Into this night I wander,
Amid the sea of awaiting dreams.
Cast upon the rocky shore,
Like pebbles on a beach.

As the wind blows,
Voices trapped in time.
Swirling as the mists conceal,
An echo in my mind.

Hollow words murmured,
Empty gestures made.
When you kiss me softly,
Moments captured, to replay.

Through closed eyes I can see you,
Perfect but not real.
Tears stream down my cheeks,
As the dawn of reality wakes.

But into the real world I stumble,
The pain melts my heart.
My mind a vortex of thoughts,
Where does it stop, where did it start.

Joe Angell (16)
Coulsdon High School

PREDATOR

Sneaking through grassy jungle,
Dew rolling off each blade.
Undetected, creeping still,
Without a single noise made.

Prey spotted in the distance!
Lying there blissfully unaware.
Would it run and hide away,
If it knew the predator was there?

Crouching down low,
Ready to pounce.
Gathering of energy,
Each and every ounce.

Springing up into the air,
Body flexed, muscles taught.
Movements sleek like panther,
The game is over! It thought.

Crashing down onto its prey,
Sudden rush, sharp blow.
Paws wrapped round the piece of string!
Pausing, my cat waits for another go.

Lorraine Reynolds (15)
Coulsdon High School

SCHOOLZ OUT

It's good to have my freedom,
It seems so long ago,
That my freedom was with me,
I hope it will never go!

It's good to be back home,
I'm staying here for a while,
I think I'll have a break now,
From all those tests and trials!

I've got to go back one day,
I can't stay here forever,
Even though tomorrow's Monday,
It's important that I'm clever.

At last back to Mum's cooking,
It tastes and smells so good,
If I could stay here for eternity,
Honestly, I really would!

My mobile is fully charged,
Lots of credit to text,
I'll look back upon my school days,
And wonder what victim's next . . .

Lee Robert Hudson (12)
Coulsdon High School

UNTITLED

A billion candles all lit at once,
A million car headlights,
The stabbing beam of a torch,
A lonely light bulb, that swings from its wire.

Guess what it is?

It searches for bodies, for shapes and souls,
And creates darkness wherever it falls,
A twinkling star that burns in the sky,
At night, at day, all round the clock,
The early riser, first off the block
It's the last thing at night to fall asleep,
It's the last to collapse in a tired heap.

Come on, you can get it. Think!

A stage light, that points only at me,
It rises over the horizon,
Like a tired body that drags itself out of bed,
After a night spent on the town.

Can you tell yet?

When it gets forty winks, so does everyone else,
Everyone who's had a tiring day,
A bad day,
A good day,
Or just a regular day in the life
Of 'Joe Normal',
He's that guy we all know,
Just a regular Joe,
He's nothing special.

But when he rises to the light of the sun,
He feels one in a million.

Mathew White (15)
Coulsdon High School

A CITY AT NIGHT

A city was scattered with rubbish bins like the gravestones
There is nobody anywhere in sight, it is like a silent desert.

Everybody is tucked up in silk sleeping like logs
People laughing like hyenas on the African plains
It is raining really hard, the moon is shining out
Onto a tidal wave bound stormy sea.

There is thunder and lightning up above
It is probably God moving his furniture in an angry mood.

Every shop is empty and as silent as a mouse
Bottle bins after them are being emptied

The busy street twists and turns like country lanes after dark
Because every light bulb to be seen has been vandalised.

Every alley is as dark as a foggy sea at night.

The silent rumble of a subway train going into South Street
Like an escaping herd of wildebeest!

The silent miaowing from the alley is a distant police siren.

Tall buildings and skyscrapers compete in the 'who is the tallest
                                                        contest'
While a man sits freezing cold sipping hot chocolate at his desk.

The distant noise of disco music coming from a local night-club
Is like the sound of jackals after a successful hunting trip.

Calum Ross (14)
Coulsdon High School

UNTITLED

How could I forget
You scarred my aching heart
The most important answers
Are those whose questions
Are never asked
But I wanted you . . .

And etched on your face
An unhappy memory
Your feelings paint a picture
Hurt and pain, you bare all
You stayed too long . . .

All behind no looking forward
Back to the past
When I had it all
Loosened my grasp
And let you fall
And now you are looking up at me
It makes no sense at all
Me with you . . .

How could I have held you
When the world wanted you
You stayed too long
'But took me with you
Hurry up and go
But don't leave
Turn away
But stop to look once more.

Rebecca Smith (15)
Coulsdon High School

RAPUNZEL!

There was one day a little girl,
Who had long hair with one big curl.
Rapunzel was locked in a tower,
On which the wicked witch had power.
Then as her 18th birthday came,
She had one present, which was her main.
It was a PlayStation with Smackdown Two,
Apart from that she had games few.
Then along came a very tall prince,
While Rapunzel was eating her mince.
'Climb up my hair!' Rapunzel called,
But then she turned just slightly bald.
'I don't want a wife who's as bald as a pig,
If I were to marry you I'd buy you a wig!'
'You useless Prince, get out of the way!'
He heard the women's institute say.
This included Sleeping Beauty and Snow White,
Not forgetting Cinderella and her kite.
'We'll save you only if you say,
You'll give us a fiver or more a day.'
Rapunzel agreed and cried, *'Yippee!*
In a moment I will be free!'
The institution abseiled up,
'Wait a min, I'll grab my cup!'
As they were on the way down,
They saw the witch give a frown,
'Oh never mind,' said the Hag,
As she began to smoke a fag.

Charlotte Bush & Charlotte Armstrong (11)
Coulsdon High School

THE END

The darkness swept around her feet,
As she trod carefully through the dirt.
Anxious to get home, afraid to meet
The man, she must be on alert.

The minutes ticked slowly by,
As she walked briskly home.
Wary of the silence, she must try,
To forget she was not alone.

The rustle of an overcoat,
She quickly turned around.
But only espying a sleeping goat,
Stretched out upon the ground.

There were definitely footsteps now,
Coming round the bend.
She had to hide somewhere, but how,
Then it was the end.

Richard Wise (15)
Coulsdon High School

AS A TREE

My branches grow throughout the years
The harsh, strong winds cause me sap tears
The birds fly among my branches
Each day they put me into trances

Quietly I'll always be listening
Secretly I'll be glistening
I want fairies to dance round me
But there will still be stinging bees

When the time comes my bark will break
It will be my trunk that they take
My inside will tell my lifeline
Every detail will be mine.

Kate Lines (14)
Coulsdon High School

YOU SAID

I believed in you,
The things you said you'd do,
I had hope in you,
Backed you all the way,
I held love for you,
Letting my heart yearn,
I felt close to you,
When you held me tight,
I had thoughts of you,
Whilst sleeping through the night,
I would have died for you,
I put up with you,
The comments that you made,
I stood up to you,
You couldn't take it that way,
I was faithful to you,
Could have chose not to be,
I was too good for you,
You were too blind to see,
I gave chances to you,
Abused them every time,

You said you loved me. . . you lied.

Nicola Kingett (15)
Coulsdon High School

THE GOOD SAMARITAN

A man was robbed
What a shame!
His clothes, his money
He was left in pain.

A man walked past
As if . . .
The victim was not in sight
A second walked past
He turned in fright.

A third walked past
And the victim thought he might
A fourth was strolling past
He saw the victim
He cleaned him fast.

He then helped him up
This was class
The Samaritan paid
For medical care.

Treatment or
The world aware
Can surpass
But has no class.

Stephanie Taylor (12)
Coulsdon High School

UNTITLED

When you are feeling down,
And everyone's let you down.

Just look up at the sky,
At the birds flying high.

And imagine yourself flying,
Just like the birds flying high.

Look at the deep blue sky,
And let your sorrows fly.

Then you feel a lot lighter,
Like your problems have been solved.

But when you are feeling happy,
And all is well with you.

Remember the sad people,
That are unhappy too.

Make a wish for them,
That they'll be happy too.

So that everyone is happy,
And all is well on earth.

Jennifer Osoata (15)
Coulsdon High School

ADVANCE ON THE BEACHHEAD

The chugging of the engine
The pounding of shells
The swaying of the boat
Rocking around in the swells

With a sudden shout
And a deafening cry
Men fell all around me
And I was hit in the side

I fell to the floor
And got out of the boat
Swam amongst the bodies
Lifeless but afloat

Regaining my senses
And shaking with fear
I crawled up the beach
Taking shelter behind the dead

Explosions all around me
People's limbs by my side
I soon began to realise
The reality of my life

Hiding from bullets
Swishing through the air
Men charging at the enemy
As if they didn't care

Reaching the relative safety
Of a sandbank shelter
I witnessed the final moments
Of people I had met just earlier

Now what happened next I do not know
But they told me I had fainted
For when I awoke with a bandaged side
I was missing one leg, but safe

I soon returned home
Disabled but grateful
My war had ended here
Not somewhere in battle.

Mark Chandler (15)
Coulsdon High School

THE SCHOOL BULLY

I run through the corridor,
I run up the stairs,
He's trying to beat me up,
To get my bus fare.

He grabbed me by my ankles,
Shakes me till I'm dazed,
To empty my pockets for my dinner money,
You know what? I think he's crazed!

I ran into the toilets,
To try and get away,
He crashed the door like a psychopath,
To say he'll make me pay.

But in the end,
I say with a grin,
A greedy, bloodthirsty bully,
Will never win!

Michael Knight (12)
Coulsdon High School

I DON'T LIKE POETS

I can't write poems,
Nothing rhymes, nothing makes any sense.
Although I do have one thing to say.
About poets, that is.
What kind of people call themselves poets anyway?
Do they get paid?
Does anyone take you seriously when at the age of sixteen
you proclaim you want to be a poet?
My stereo-typical idea of a poet,
Is a man/woman - tweed, anoraks and ponchos,
For those long walks, they take in the middle of nowhere!
They sit and ponder,
Sit and wonder,
(There that rhymed!)
Hair is bad, dark circles under eyes,
The local poet society, clicking fingers?
Black coffee.
No,
Poets don't do it for me,
I don't think I'll marry a poet.

Amy Lines (16)
Coulsdon High School

END OF DAY

In my house I sit
listening to the muffled sounds next door.
My sister's in her room singing
I try hard to ignore.

Smells from the kitchen waft upstairs
it makes my taste buds tingle.
The children outside are playing dares
as the ice cream bell jingles.

The yellow sunlight begins to fall
as the sun begins to set.
The light casts shadows on my wall
as I snuggle up to my pet.

This is how the day has ended.
Tomorrow I will start again.

Natalie Mills (15)
Coulsdon High School

WHO IS GOD?

Who is God I ask myself,
And what part does he play on this Earth?
We pray, we talk and ask of him
Solutions to our problems;
World peace,
Good health,
Or simply love.
Who is God I ask myself?
A football star, a movie star,
A surgeon or a doctor,
A man, a woman,
Or the image taught to us through religion?
The creator,
The ruler,
A supreme being.
Who is God I ask myself?
For everyone it is different,
Or
Is there really a God at all?
Questions with so many answers.

Christos Nicoli (15)
Coulsdon High School

MY FRIEND HOLLIE

The love I have for my friend
Is a love I know will never end
Even though she's been taken afar
I look up and see her shining through a star
The day she was taken I'll never forget
It made me remember the day we had met
I closed my eyes and saw that big cheeky smile
The one that could beam for mile upon mile
To think I would never see it again
Brought me to tears and brings so much pain
I miss my friend so very much
Her laugh, her voice and her gentle touch
I hope she is happy wherever she is
And knows she is loved and very, very missed.

Natalie Edwards (15)
Coulsdon High School

NIGHTMARES

Coats blacker than night
Drenched in sweat
Their fiery, red eyes roll
And hooves of iron send sparks flying
Galloping like possessed race horses
Devils crouched low over their backs
Kicking and beating them on
Their breath as hot as a furnace
As it escapes their blood-red nostrils

As morning comes they will vanish
Until the night when they return to haunt you.

Bethan Stacey (12)
Coulsdon High School

TRUE, SIMPLE

Death is simple,
Love is true,
But neither are always to be.

Death comes when you're old,
Death comes when you're young,
But you never know when it will be.

But love comes now,
And love comes then,
And you'll know when it's there somehow,
For the hum of a bee,
And the whisper of wind will float your heart on clouds.

Niomie Heather Slater (11)
Coulsdon High School

MY DOG

How pretty she is,
Running in the field.
Her soft black fur,
Shimmering in the sun.

She lifts her head to smell the warm air,
Then looks at me with her face full of excitement.
Does she really know how much grace she has in her step?
And that she runs as a soft owl flies?

As the rays of sun catch her coat,
She stops as I call her name.
After a while she comes running up,
So that we can go home again.

Charlotte Surridge (13)
Dunottar School

THE WHALE AND THE LITTLE FISH

The whale swims from side to side,
His massive mouth has opened wide.
Swim little fish, swim, swim, swim,
Oh no, it's too late, the whale will win.

The whale's fish is in his suck
But suddenly he screams, 'Yuck, yuck, yuck.'
He blows through his spout
And spits the fish out.

And then he says through a mouthful of weed,
'My gosh, my gosh, what is that breed?'
And so the fish says through a mouthful of gob,
'Please don't laugh but I'm a blob.'

The whale gives a look of disgust
Then swims away without any thrust.
And then the fish thinks 'It's a lucky thing,
That whale will just believe anything.'

Clare E Reeves (11)
Dunottar School

THE STORMY SEA

All the animals are swimming under the waves,
The sea is crashing on the shore,
On a dark and stormy night,
The rain is pouring down tip-tap, tip-tap,
Like an ice cream in the sun dripping down the cone.

The wind is whistling as it rushes past,
Moving the trees backwards and forwards,
Then abruptly comes the thunder,
Crash, bang, crash, bang, and rumbling together.

Here I am sitting indoors,
Watching everyone outside sadly suffer,
And I'm here with a fire crackling all cosy and warm.
Finally the treacherous storm is over,
And it is gladly moving away.

Victoria White (11)
Dunottar School

NIGHTMARE

A distant bell tolls midnight, a most treacherous hour,
When the evil of creation is at its height of power.

A lost man with no lantern, stumbles through a street,
Lurching through a graveyard, heavy on his feet.

A grave slab opens slowly to show a withered hand,
And then the crumbling body of what was once a man.

All the dead are rising, like prisoners from their tomb,
To do their master's bidding born from evil's womb.

The man is soon surrounded by death on every side,
Nowhere can he run to, nowhere can he hide.

Their hands are grabbing at him, their stench of dirt and must.
His screams pierce every eardrum, but his foes turn into dust.

And then he sees the angel, a glow in blackened skies
The source of his salvation that saved him from demise.

He wakes up in the gutter, remembering his dream,
Remembering the angel, remembering his scream.

Thankful for the daylight, thankful for the sun,
Vowing to remember to give up all the rum.

Sarah-Louise Jordan (13)
Dunottar School

PEACE

There is nothing greater than this,
It is the wish of each and every man,
The silver lining of the gloomy and
Lingering cloud of war;
Pure harmony between all nations,
All races, creeds and colours.

It is an extended friendship
Including everyone,
Perfect describes how life would be,
Its light would envelop the whole world
And its peoples for eternity.

We should strive to achieve it
As much as we can,
'It starts at home' is the saying
So let it begin with me and you.

The world is wounded and
We must try to heal it,
Then will come the sunshine
After this long spell of rain.

The Earth would be a better planet
For all to live in;
No more war,
No suffering,
Eternal bliss.
Peace.

Natasha Kay (13)
Dunottar School

WITCH GIRL

No one understands me
The way I choose to live
My family thinks it's evil
They think that I should give.

Not take away from humans
I say I'm human too,
But they say I'm a monster
They just don't have a clue.

They say that I am voodoo
I use my magic to kill,
But all I do is help things
Using my gift and skill.

The world is so confusing
Its pieces torn apart,
So why do we destroy life?
This intricately painted art.

This art is reproducing
This art is setting free
This world of devastation
The art just hasn't reached me.

My parents think I'm ugly
The way I dress and look.
My friends say it's 'real cool'
When I use my magic book.

I've chosen to live this way
I will not change my mind,
No fairy tale this magic
This magic that I find.

Hebe Jones (11)
Dunottar School

MY PERFECT PET

I've been thinking for ages of a pet to buy,
First I thought about a cat,
But a cat needs too much feeding,
And I wouldn't want to do that.

Then I thought of a rabbit,
The great big fluffy things,
But then I thought of the cage to buy.
So I thought I wouldn't give it a try.

I've also thought of a dog.
Yes, that would be a good idea.
But I'm too lazy to give it walks,
So I think I'll try a frog.

I thought a frog would be the thing,
It just hops and jumps all day,
But when it croaked I screamed too loud,
So it leapt away.

But now I've got the perfect pet,
It doesn't need feeding or walking,
All day long it sits on my chair,
It is my teddy bear.

Catherine Jenkins (12)
Dunottar School

THE CLOUD

I am a little cloud,
I flit across the sky,
I look white when it's sunny,
And people love me when it's dry.

But when it's dark and windy,
And rain is pouring down,
You'll look up and curse me,
And give a little frown.

Charlotte Luke (11)
Dunottar School

HALLOWE'EN

There is a chill in the air,
And the moon is full.
Should you even dare,
To think of ghosts and ghouls?

There's a shadow in the hall,
Is your mind playing games?
You hear a frightening call,
Shouting your name.

You're in the house on your own,
All the doors are locked.
You keep hearing creaks and moans,
And your door's being knocked.

As quiet as a mouse,
As scared as a cat,
You move through the house,
As quick as a rat.

You can hear shrieks and laughter,
Behind the door outside.
It's just trick or treaters,
There's no need to hide.

Annabel Hook (12)
Dunottar School

THE PICTURE

As I open my eyes in the morning,
The first thing I see is a picture
Full of happiness and memories.
Her smile of joy, illuminating everything near her,
Eyes sparkling like jewels.
I can hear the trickling of water,
And the chirping of birds,
Floods of laughter fill my ears.
An endless multicoloured sea of flowers surrounds us.
At that moment in time nothing on Earth matters to us,
We don't have a care in the world,
All we know is that we are together
Enjoying this beautiful summer's day,
With the sun beating down on us.
How could I have known,
That soon my whole world would shatter like glass?
I manage to tear myself away from the photograph
And wipe away my tears.
The only words I can hear are 'It's not your fault.'
I know now that she hasn't left,
But is just watching from a different plane.
Guiding me through life, through my thoughts and dreams,
My guardian angel, protecting me from harm,
And as I open my eyes in the morning,
The first thing I see is a picture,
Full of happiness and memories
Which I will never forget and keep close to my heart forever.

Marie-Claire Wyatt (14)
Dunottar School

MY CAT

Crouching low, hidden by grass,
The black predator, swift and fast.
Stalking, seeking, his emerald eyes,
Glowing, glinting, gleaming wide.

He pauses, silent, his heart beating fast,
Watching the squirrel who's near at last.
All at once like a rocket he launches forward,
But misses his chance as the squirrel escapes.

Annoyed at his failure, he stalks back inside,
Yet still energetic, looks for something that hides,
Maybe a mouse, or even a rat,
Nothing's too big for my clever cat.

Then he spies his next target, alone by herself,
She lives in a bowl, that sits on a shelf.
She has a gold costume and large pursing lips,
She swims round in circles, but don't hold her, she'll slip!

He circles the kitchen, head in the air,
He jumps on the table, with a great deal of care.
He licks his lips and gives a miaow,
But Mum comes along and he's put on the ground!

He retreats to his basket, in defeat.
Oh how he longs for some meat,
But the meat that he gets, comes from a tin,
Well at least, he can catch something!

Sophie Robinson (13)
Dunottar School

MEMORIES OF MY GRANDPA

My grandpa was special
His needs were not great
He needed his family
Scrumptious food on a plate.

He sang in the mornings
His heart was aglow
Some enchanted evening
Was always aflow.

His mischievous humour
His face in a smirk
He'd be cheeky to the nurses
And they'd laugh like Pauline Quirk.

The card games we played
He never would cheat
He'd play for hours and hours
In the same old seat.

Grandpa watched me at riding
He spoke words of advice
To assistants he'd say, 'Much obliged to you!'
He was rather too nice.

Grandpa enjoyed his crosswords
He might ask for my help
He'd play with Amber for ages
He'd grab the ball and she'd yelp.

However 'Grandpa the person'
Was whom I loved best.
He has gone up to be with Nanny
His lovely heart is at rest.

Maxime Sabatini (13)
Dunottar School

THE WIND

The wind is there,
It's like an invisible man,
Creeping everywhere.

It rattles the windowpanes,
It knocks down a vase.
It whistles through the keyholes,
It breaks the jars.

It blows on the doors,
And makes them creak.
It sweeps round the house,
And makes the mice squeak.

When I'm lying in bed,
On a cold winter's night.
The invisible man,
Comes to fight.

I shiver and shake,
In the bed that I lie.
I try to keep warm,
I really do try.

Laura Spicer (11)
Dunouar School

CHUMP

There once was a horse called Chump,
He always loves to jump.
When he gets back,
He eats till he's fat,
That is how he gets so plump.

Julia Scott (11)
Dunottar School

AMERICA'S DISASTER

Planes crashing,
Years blown away in seconds,
Who on Earth would do this?

So much destruction,
Buildings once gleaming
Collapsed before our eyes.

Many people jumped out of windows
Others fled to the stairs,
Brave firemen raced to the inferno,
To try and save some lives,
So few came out alive.

Families clutching pictures
Searched the streets.
Sadly most were cremated in the
Fireball we once knew as the
Twin Towers.

Erica Norton (13)
Dunottar School

THE LOSS OF LIFE

The day the Devil came
Many people went insane.
The two both came crashing down
Like a distant memory revived once again.
People screaming
Lost in dust,
Pieces of glass shattered the floor.

The thousands of windows glisten no more,
The hundreds of people that died
Will remain
In our hearts.
The twin towers
Standing tall
Have fallen and live there no more.

Grace Roberts (12)
Dunottar School

COLOURS

Colours are the strangest things
They vary from white to black.
Some colours can be very light,
While others may attack.

Each person has a favourite one.
It changes from year to year.
The yellow sun, the orange leaves,
The white snow that sheds a tear.

These things called colours,
I am able to relate,
To my deepest emotions,
Like love and hate.

The colours may all combine,
In a mixing bowl of fire.
As you look for the pot of gold,
The rainbow can get higher and higher.

Alice Whitney (13)
Dunottar School

THE GHOST AT IVY HOUSE

There's a ghost at Ivy House
There is a scary mouse.
But most of all that scares me is . . .
. . . The ghost at Ivy House.

The creeping on the stairs,
The whistling through my hair,
The slamming of the doors,
The walking in the halls.

The prickles at the back of my neck,
The rocking of the chair.

And all these terrifying things are from . . .

. . . The ghost at Ivy House.

Stephanie Young (11)
Dunottar School

THE FIRE

The fire was blazing,
My brother was playing.
I was trying to get warm.

My dad was searching,
My brother was perching.
My dad found the wood.

The fire was beaming,
I started screaming
And my brother was there no more.

Emily Gemma Haynes (12)
Dunottar School

THE SUN

Ever since the day I was born
The sun comes out every morn,
It comes out every single day
It really takes my breath away.
It shines so bright, that orange ball
In the air, one million feet tall,
It never does come out at night
But when it comes out, it's really bright.
It reflects the colours red, blue and white
Those lovely bright spots of light.
It goes down in the evening and
Flows away into the night.

Alex Barron (12)
Dunottar School

DOGS

Dogs come in all different shapes and sizes.
There are lots of different kinds
Alsatian, Dalmatian and collie
They are so clever.
The way they know sit, stay and lay
You'll never guess what I've got.
She's brown, black and white
She's a German Shepherd call Reg
And I love her to bits
She plays, eats, jumps and runs
All day long.

Kimberley-Jayne Stoneman (12)
Dunottar School

THE GOOSE, HIS MATE AND THEIR FRIEND

Every day they fly the same pathway,
The goose, his mate and their friend.
Strong wings beating the rhythm of the journey,
Until they reach the familiar end.

Today they pass over a field,
Where the indiscriminate killers wait.
He feels the searing heat in his thigh,
As he calls to his falling mate.

She's now in a field far away,
There's no water where she's lying.
Peppered with shot, she is breathing hard,
The long process of dying.

Evening comes, she is drifting now,
As she hears the familiar shout.
From up in the sky as they pass overhead,
But her lifeblood is pouring out.

She wants to be with them, her mate and their friend,
But her freedom was taken away
By a fool with a shotgun and no conscience,
And indifferent to nature's way.

The goose and his friend cannot see her,
She's less than a speck down below.
She cannot reply to his questioning cry,
She is biding her time till she goes.

The last thing she sees are the two flying geese,
As her life reaches its premature end.
But her spirit will rise in the autumn skies,
To join the goose and his friend.

Emily Skinner (12)
Dunottar School

THE HEADMISTRESS WANTS TO SEE ME

I knock on the door and walk right in,
It really isn't fair.
I don't know what I've done
But I'm in the head teacher's lair.

She sits behind her massive desk,
Perched upon her chair.
She looks over the bridge of her glasses,
With a very spiteful glare.

'Do you know why you're in here?'
She growls like a hungry wolf,
I shiver and shake and open my mouth,
But am far too scared to talk.

I look at her face that's staring down,
There's a huge hairy wart on her chin.
Her eyebrows hang into her eyes,
Her lips are mean and thin.

She's six feet tall and five feet wide,
There's a tight brown bun on her head.
Wiry glasses rest on her nose,
Her eyes are the colour of lead.

'I'm told you like to talk a lot,
And do it all the time.'
I wanted to defend myself,
But really felt like crying.

'You're to come to school on Open Day.'
I started to protest.
'You'll show the parents round the school,
And have Monday off to rest.'

Rachel Collum (11)
Dunottar School

FOOT AND MOUTH

The wind was a whirl of darkness under the shadowy night,
The trees were a shiver of horror over the dead bodies,
The grass was a dirty mess,
When a hawk came swooping by
Swooping, swooping, swooping
Over the heap of death.

He had a white, white suit
All splattered with blood
And some goggles upon his head.
His patients not cured but killed
When a tractor came bumpily past.
Bumpily, bumpily, bumpily
When a tractor came bumpily past.

Arriving next morning to inject the lambs
He knocked hard at our farm gate
But I wouldn't let him in
I just couldn't let him in
For I knew what he would do if I let him in.
So I turned him away.

Jessica Jones (11)
Dunottar School

HAPPY THOUGHTS

Once in life there came to me,
A maid pure and sweet as could be.
But I trust that she's for me,
And will never fail or leave me,
But will one day in my life
Become my true and faithful one.

Natasha Mitchell (12)
Dunottar School

LONELINESS

I was lonely one day,
all alone on the bench,
sitting there with no one to play with,
someone came up to me and called me a squirt.

I was alone in my bedroom,
sitting there with no one,
someone came up to me and said something,
I didn't understand.

I walked to school all alone,
no one to walk with,
no one to talk with,
someone came up to me and said 'Don't walk on your own.'

I was at the park,
all alone, swinging on a swing,
no one to play with,
no one to swing with,
I was all alone,
swinging there, swinging there, swinging there.

It was cold and frosty,
and a man was shivering,
the leaves were crackling,
the bells were rattling,
the clouds were grey,
I walked around, all alone, alone, alone!

Eleanor Rae (11)
Dunottar School

CONFUSION

When I was a baby
I heard everyone talking
Talking, talking, talking about me.
I didn't understand.
I was confused.
I felt confused.

I went to school on the very first day.
I was alone.
I had no friends.
Everything was big.
Everything was tall.
I was confused.
I felt confused.

At home, I am taught to listen,
Not to do as I do,
But to do as I say,
I was small and they were tall.
I was confused.
I felt confused.

I ate my dinner because I
Was told that I must,
Greens and sprouts and all that's raw.
My mum said they were good for me,
But I'm a young girl and sweets give me energy,
My dentists said they were bad for me
And plenty of fruit and veg were what I needed
I was confused.
I felt confused.

Today I watch the news,
And see people killing each other,
Adults being cruel to children,
People hating each other because of colour,
Hospitals that are too full,
Schools that are struggling,
All in the new better world,
I am confused.
I feel confused.

Natasha Bhana (10)
Dunottar School

WHERE ARE THOSE TWIN TOWERS?

Thousands of lives lost
As those towers came crashing down.
Innocent people called
Their loved ones
Saying their last goodbyes.
Those terrorists who caused
Such disaster to the world.
It's weird to think
That only just over a month ago
They were standing bold.
The World Trade Center
Is no longer there, because of
Those terrible people
Who don't have anything better to do
Than kill themselves
And other people too.
Manhattan has been battered
But the whole world has been shattered.

Abigail Watson (12)
Dunottar School

WHEN THE CHURCH BELLS RING AT MIDNIGHT

As the ghostly hour draws near,
And the church bell in the graveyard rings
By immortal hands,
And the pale, watery moon sails sadly
Across the stormy sky,
A faint rumble of thunder can be heard
Far away.
And the forked lightning strikes as
Though it's pierced the sky and hits the
Dismal graveyard as if cursing it.
A strong wind would shiver down your
Spine making you cold and uneasy,
The faded gravestones, chipped and worn
With age, stand motionless and lifeless
In the bleak desolate yard.
Slime and moss cling to them and grime covers them.
Just as the bell has finished ringing for the twelfth time,
A high-pitched drone, which sounds as
Though the world will split in two,
Will ring through your ears making your
Head spin and your blood will run cold.
This is followed by a deadly silence,
And then the cold windy night, is filled
With the deadly, echoing chant of unearthly creatures,
They appear from the underworld, screeching
And wailing
Leading the procession is no one other
Than the Devil himself.
Who perches himself on a tombstone
To watch the mysterious terrifying creatures
Dance round the gravestones.

Witches with pointed hats, goblins,
Wicked fairies, ghosts and spirits prance
Round the churchyard enjoying themselves,
They dance to a sombre eerie drone
That is sung by the Devil
And the noise would make anyone cringe.
But as the night fades away and the
Sun is just rising,
Sending warm rays rushing down to Earth.
The immortal creatures led
By the Devil
Vanish into thin air . . .
Until tomorrow night.

Jenny Stevens (13)
Dunottar School

THE CIRCUS

The circus is coming to town!
The circus is coming to town!

Lions roar like thunder,
Tigers' stripes so bright with colour.

The circus is coming to town!
The circus is coming to town!

Clowns are coming with their jokes and pranks,
Dogs are coming to perform tricks.

The circus is here!
The circus is here!

Verity Marie Lambert (11)
Dunottar School

SEASONS

Autumn is a time of fluttering leaves,
Red, gold and brown ones part the trees.
The moon starts to shine as the evening ends,
We now know it's autumn,
No pretends.

Empty branches are cold and wet,
As the leaves have drifted away.
The sun has gone, it's lost its power,
We're coming to the end of the day.

Spring is a time of new, new life,
Because many animals are born.
The trees and flowers blossom,
And the old sheep are shorn.

Summer is a time of sunbathing,
For now it's nice and hot.
While the sheep are in the field grazing,
Autumn is on the trot.

Georgina Wilkins (11)
Dunottar School

THE EAGLE

The eagle soars across the sky,
She's searching for her prey.
The tiny field mouse runs below,
He's trying to get away.

The eagle quickly dives now,
She's nearly won the chase.
The mouse's utter exhaustion,
Is slowing down his pace.

But now the game is over,
The eagle has won her prey.
The eagle's stomach is full now,
Until the next day.

Hannah Liddle (12)
Dunottar School

MY WINDOW

As I gaze through my window,
I glimpse the first break of the day,
The first flutter of a phoenix
On its journey away.

As I gaze through my window,
I peer at the lights,
That flood heavily down from all heights.

As I gaze through my window,
I glare at the green grass,
Swaying in rhythm with the wind that does pass.

As I gaze through my window,
I watch them glide,
The golden leaves
In and out of each other they do weave.

As I gaze through my window,
I see the beautiful colours,
Of a butterfly's wing
They are so bright and shiny
They make your eyes sting.

As gaze through my window
I see the world as it is,
Warm . . . comfortable . . . and bliss.

Katie Hamilton (13)
Dunottar School

SWEETS, SWEETS, *SWEETS!*

The sweets were on the table,
As I came in from the stable.
There were big ones, small ones,
Long ones and tall ones,
And they were waiting to be eaten-eaten-eaten,
And they were waiting to be eaten all up.

As Dad was mowing the lawn,
And Mum was picking some corn.
I sneaked a sweet from the jar,
It tasted like a Milky Way star.
It felt like it was going to explode-explode-explode,
And it felt like it was going to explode right inside my mouth.

I could not believe my luck, for these chocolates were so yummy,
And there were so many in my tummy-tummy-tummy,
And there were so many in my tummy and mouth.

After a while I did not feel well,
For my tummy was starting to ring its bell.
Never again will I eat so much chocolate,
For those sweets-sweet-sweets,
For those sweets are so annoying!

Katie Holden (11)
Dunottar School

THE LADY WHO SAT DEAD STILL

There was an old lady from Redhill,
Who always sat dead still,
She never ate a thing,
So a wasp gave her a sting,
And now she never sits still.

Misba Rashid (11)
Dunottar School

11TH SEPTEMBER, 911

In the morning I woke up
had a shower and got dressed,
I went downstairs to have my breakfast
It seemed like a normal day.

Said 'Goodbye' to my wife and kids,
and walked out the door.
Said 'Hello' to the construction workers,
and kept walking on.

I felt in my pocket to see my cell phone
It wasn't there!
I turned back to the house
the kids were there.
I gave them a kiss and grabbed my phone
and walked out again.

It was 8.47 and all was well,
I strolled in right on time.
50th floor, I'm so high up
Brrring, brring, my friend from Britain.

The phone cut off . . . I heard a bang
The 60th floor was gone!
I ran to the stairs as fast as I could
Tick-tock, tick-tock
Time went by, I was on the 10th floor
Not close enough, a traffic jam of people.

Tumble, tumble, tumble!
I was on the ground with beams on me,
My cell phone was vibrating
I tried to get it, but I just couldn't
And then the pain stopped
And it was dark.

Francoise Trappey (12)
Dunottar School

LEGEND

(Based on the poem 'Legend' by Judith Wright)

I went on a journey once
To the Grand Emperor's Court
Where everything weighed an ounce
And the queen lived in the fort.

The castle floor was made of pink glass
And the ceilings made of paper,
The walls were painted purple and brass
And there lived the Emperor.

There was a greenhouse in the garden
It was filled with vanity and pride.
The flowers were made of argent
And the princess lived inside.

The prince lived in a chapel
With lots of other monks
For his dinner he ate an apple
And bite-sized chicken chunks.

Their house was built expertly
But their lives were round the bend
There they lived separately
In a complete and utter legend.

Emma Burvill (12)
Dunottar School

STARS

Stars glowing shining bright
In the very cold nights.
Winter's here and all is dark
Apart from all the little stars.

Stars are faint and hardly seen
In the warm and mysterious wind,
Summer's here and all is light,
Apart from the dark nights.

Ruth Munroe (13)
Dunottar School

BAD DAY

Dear . . .

It was such a boring day
There was nothing to do nor play
And it was chucking it down with rain

I got a letter, hope it's better
Than this boring bad day.
It said I had to pay a fine
Because I'd stepped over the line
The line from Mr Brian's garden
I didn't know what to say but 'Pardon!'

With my black boots of leather
This is worse than the weather
No wonder they are dirty,
Oh, I thought they were flirty!

How much did I have to pay?
Good Lord, a hundred pounds a day!
That's a lot to have to pay -
This really isn't my day!

Kirina Wright (13)
Dunottar School

HOMELESS

I was walking down a street,
by a starving child sitting on the floor.
She was wrapped in a blanket,
blanket, blanket
She was wrapped in a blanket sitting on the floor.

She had a little hat,
Which had only a couple of pennies in
So I bent right down and popped two pounds in.
She wriggled slowly and peered right in,
In amazement, she picked it up carefully
carefully, carefully.
She picked it up carefully in her dark muffled skin

She hid in her blanket,
she looked puzzled and scared.
I don't think she knew what it was,
but then she looked and stared like joy was ringing
in her heart.
'Thanks,' she said in a whisper but then disappeared

disappeared, disappeared with not a sound at all.

Sophie O'Connor (11)
Dunottar School

THE DREAM

Clouds of thoughtless wonder,
Drift across my mind,
I fall into a hypnotic sleep,
And everything is left behind.

My worries, troubles and disasters,
I can see no more,
But I can look at happiness wandering towards me,
And I will never tire.

People singing and dancing,
Smiles across their faces,
An angelic song floats through the air.
The sound is like a bird singing its joyful tune.

The trance has ended now,
There is no going back,
To the happy place up above,
That I have always loved.

Eleanor Wells (10)
Dunottar School

THE PLUMBER AND THE PRINCESS

The sun was as bright as fire, the sky was as blue as the Caribbean Sea,
The apples on the tree were crispy and juicy
And the plumber was working - working - working,
The plumber kept on working till noon was on its way.

A princess walked on by, her dress as gold as autumn leaves,
Her long jet-black hair blowing and swaying in the wind,
Her red lips glowing and her blue eyes twinkling - twinkling -
twinkling,
Her blue eyes twinkling at the plumber whilst he worked.

They went for a meal and carried on meeting each other,
The princess was afraid her father, the King, would find out
But she carried on seeing the plumber.
The prince was jealous and he told the King,
The princess's heart was pounding - pounding - pounding,
Her heart pounded, for her father had locked her in a cell.

Caroline Drew (11)
Dunottar School

DEATH

The Angels of Death came nearer
Wearing their blood-stained clothes
Ready to kill some more
All the lonely cattle
Grazing in the field
If only they knew
They knew, they knew
If only they knew
What was going to happen

Angels of Death are watching
Choosing their next victim
Getting their guns ready and aiming
Aiming, aiming
Getting their guns ready and aiming
Bang!

Angels of Death are walking
Walking all around
Mountains of ash around them
Choking them with their guilt
Their guilt, their guilt
Choking them with their guilt
It's all their fault

Angels of Death are choking
The smell of perfume doesn't cover
The smell of death
The smell of death never goes
Never goes, never goes
The smell of death never goes
It's always in the air

The farmers are all crying
Angels of Death are wondering
If what they did was right
Was right, was right.

Calandra Stone (11)
Dunottar School

NELSON MANDELA IN HIS CELL

I was sitting in my cell waiting,
With no one by my side,
I wanted someone there -
There - there -
I wanted someone there, with me.

Suddenly my door opened,
I thought my time had come,
But I was wrong -
Wrong - wrong -
But I was wrong, I still had many years to go.

All it was, was my water, porridge and salad,
It was the food that made me sick,
I knew I couldn't because I needed the food -
Food - food -
I knew I couldn't because, I needed the food and I had to
live it out.

Five years on,
And I'm free but no one understands,
But now I'm happy and no one can stop that,
Except *me!*

Stephanie Gibson (11)
Dunottar School

A Prisoner Of War

I was running round the battlefield puffing like a dog,
An enemy ran in front of me sprinting like a lion,
I pulled the trigger of my gun,
The bang almost deafened me,
The enemy collapsed slowly,
                 slowly, slowly,
The enemy collapsed slowly and drenched the ground in his blood.

Shocked and pleased, I had killed him,
Happiness was ringing in my heart,
But the enemy's friends caught me, seen what I'd done,
They dragged me,
     dragged me, dragged me,
The enemies dragged me to their van.

Over the field the van wobbled and swayed,
Along the road it trundled and chugged,
It suddenly stopped in the middle of nowhere,
And the enemies threw me,
            threw me, threw me,
The enemies threw me into a cell.

The cell was as cold as the North Pole,
It stank like a little skunk's tail,
I ran up and rattled the metal bars,
And I am waiting,
            waiting, waiting,
I am waiting to be set free.

Charlotte Main (11)
Dunottar School

SWEETS GALORE

I lay in bed one night last year
Filled with hope, apprehension and fear
I was starving hungry, one hundred percent
I wish I was in the sweet shop in Kent
I crept downstairs and out into the kitchen
And opened some tins
Baked beans, *yuck!*
Why, oh why does she buy such muck?
But soon I struck the golden prize
I found ten KitKats of monstrous size
I ate all ten and found two Mars bars
And three packets of Magic Stars
I ate my way through half and spotted my goal
The jelly belly beans!
All the flavours of my wildest dreams!
There was lemon drop, coconut, pear and plum
I devoured them all, oh what fun!
Fig, grape, tutti-frutti and soda
Then I found a cherry-cola
Honey biscuit, margarita and root beer
Then suddenly footsteps filled me with fear.
But it was only Spot the dog, and he made his mission very clear
He finished off the Mars bars and started on a Twix but soon
                                          the cockerel sounded
And I knew I would be grounded
So I slipped back into bed
And slept till half-past nine!

Katie Jillings (11)
Dunottar School

LOST!

It was a dark night
with no light in sight.
Not even a glimmer from the moon.

I was walking alone,
trying to find my way home.
But I was lost in the dark,
nowhere to walk.

I didn't know which way to go,
although the park
wasn't far from my home.

My house was in darkness
no noise at all
but a lone owl in a tree
over the see-saw!

What's that over there?
Could it be a bear,
or a wolf maybe
coming out of that tree?

All I could see were two bright eyes
and a black shadow
looking straight at me!

Look! There's a light
from a window up there.
But I didn't stay to stand and stare!

I ran towards it, though my toes were numb,
that didn't override
the thought of seeing my mum!

At last I was home, not long after that
I jumped straight into my bed
with my little black and white cat.

Laura Clemson (13)
Dunottar School

I HAVE A DREAM OF PARADISE

My biggest dream of all
Is of a paradise
Where everyone is kind and very, very nice
There are no wars and fighting;
Only the blazing and lighting,
Of the kitchen fire warmingly inviting you in

The grass is very green
And ripples in the wind
The sky is deepest blue
In a shade that cannot be dimmed
And the sun always shines
Like a mountain of twinkling gold in the morning

This paradise on Earth is a place I feel
Where dreams come true
And fantasies are real
Where sickness and hunger are
Things of the past
Where happiness and laughter
Will forever last.

Carlie Cheall (11)
Dunottar School

POEM BASED ON 'LEGEND'

A sweet young girl with fair hair
As the Legend goes, lives in a lair,
One bright day a young short lad,
Went into her lair for a dare.

The sweet young girl did not shout
Or stamp and wail 'Get out!'
She simply said 'You can go up to bed.
There is nobody here who will hurt you.'

The girl then said in an off-hand voice,
As if she had just remembered . . .
'Now you have entered you may never leave,
If you did we would both be surrendered
To the evil side who want no good,
And could, if we left, make light darkness.'

The small young boy started yelling in fright,
And he ran toward the door
The young girl tried to stop him and
She shouted even more.
But his hand had turned the handle
And her heart burned to the core.

She flung her hands up to her throat
And fell onto the floor.
There was a great yellow crack of lightning
And the clouds began to draw
A voice was whispering in her head
And then she heard no more.

Her spirit lifted from the ground
And flew up into the sky,
She saw the world below her
And was glad to say goodbye.

Some people say that this girl has caused
The dark cold ebony night,
And her spirit lies inside the moon
And every day takes that flight
Across the sky as a shooting star,
As bright as shimmering light.

Lisa Kerr (12)
Dunottar School

THE FIGHT

I heard the voices rise,
Tried to block it out.
Wishing for it to stop soon,
Wishing, wishing,
Wishing for it to stop soon
Before the lights went out.

Blocking it out didn't work,
I listened to them scream,
Words of terror and darkness,
Not hope but terror and darkness,
Under my feet they bellowed,
Under my feet they screamed.

The dark of the night was grim with dread,
The crying kept on and on,
Then suddenly stopped,
Upstairs she clattered,
The wild music started,
She sang as loud as she could.
Words of terror and darkness,
Not hope but terror and darkness,
Talk of death and hell as the lights went out.

Frances Andrews (11)
Dunottar School

LEGEND

(Based on 'Legend' by Judith Wright)

A brave young maiden went out on a mission,
Her white kitten running behind,
Into a graveyard where bats shrieked,
And ghosts wailed,
But still she walked on bravely.

Her white kitten turned suddenly grey,
A devil sat, playing his fiddle,
Mysteriously, graves lifted,
And carcasses danced eerily,
But still she walked on bravely.

Suddenly a barn owl screeched,
Her bag was taken, creepy!
Skeletons rattled,
And black crows battled,
But still she walked on bravely.

There was soon bright, hot sunshine,
Multicoloured, with some gold,
The devils turned to angels,
The skeletons fell asleep,
And still she skipped on merrily.

The graveyard was as calm as a meadow,
And happily she wandered home,
The ghosts had melted,
The witches were kind,
And still she skipped on merrily.

Jennifer Ramsdale (12)
Dunottar School

THE BLACKSMITH'S BOY

The blacksmith's boy went out, barely ten,
With visions of swinging a rainbow from his shoulder,
And people would praise and admire him,
Nobody could be bolder.

'I've got to be brave,' he said out loud,
And he looked timidly up.
But his heart was made, his mind was set,
Yet his courage could fit in a cup.

I can climb this mountain, and I will
He thought, whilst running very fast.
So he dodged rocks and climbed hills,
But took no notice of what he passed.

Night was drawing closer, nothing could be seen,
But the blacksmith's boy just ran faster.
In the midst of black and green
'I need to get home to my master!'

At the top of the hill stood the rainbow
As proud as any bear.
Its glorious light shone through the black,
And the boy stumbled up to it, with care.

Finally he reached it
And looked around proudly.
He bowed to invisible men,
Nobody could call him cowardly.

Catherine Hyatt (13)
Dunottar School

A GREAT LIFE

I know all things must die,
every plant,
every bird,
every fish,
every tree
every person
every animal
and even the tiniest insect.

We lose loved ones all the time,
it's hard I know.
We must go on,
things just can't stop
even without them.

Why don't we make the most of their time
and not waste it?
Maybe they've gone from life
but no matter what . . .
they've not gone
from our
hearts.

Denali Meyers (12)
Dunottar School

I WILL . . .

I am going on a long journey,
To a faraway land,
From the mountains and seas,
To the distant desert sands.

I will go where the winds take me,
I will climb the tallest trees,
I will fight the strongest bear,
And swim the Seven Seas.

I will sleep under the stars,
I will drink from the springs,
I will walk any distance,
And conquer all the kings.

I will do this with my bare hands,
With nothing to protect me,
I will do this one day,
You wait and see.

Janhavi Rane (12)
Dunottar School

WHERE'S THE PILL?

I am sitting on my bed
With my hand upon my head.
I feel quite ill
I need to get a pill.
I have spots on my face,
And I have just tripped over my lace.

I am rolling down the stairs
And I nearly hit my head on the chairs.
I scream and shout
But no one is about.
I walk around
But nothing I found.

I put the TV on
And made up a little song.
I scream and shout,
But nothing came out
In the end I found the pill
Guess what? . . . I don't feel ill!

Chloe Tangney (12)
Dunottar School

'LEGEND' . . . FROM THE DOG'S POINT OF VIEW
(Based on the poem 'Legend')

I ran beside the blacksmith's boy
Not sure where I was going
I ran over cobwebs, thorns and branches
I dodged the spiders everywhere
And I swam through the cold river flowing.

The sky turned black
I felt sort of scared
But I continued running beside the boy
I knew he was brave and I was not
But I don't think he cared.

He wouldn't stop running
He had determination
Mountains seemed to jump aside
Rocks rolled out of his way
He still kept going with anticipation.

The rain raced down
I was wet and cold
But I was still eager to follow him
I would not leave his side
He was really bold.

The crow called out the boy would die.
The end of the day was starting to come,
But I was worn out and could run no longer
I gave up and got lost
It wasn't fun.

I missed the blacksmith's boy
I waited all alone,
Then lay in the darkness
Waiting for someone to find me
All I wanted was to be home
But still I lay there on my own.

Hattie Ellis (12)
Dunottar School

THE LAKE

As I went in the lake
The water was swishing to and fro,
It was like stepping into an ice-cold picture
With all the wake splashing around you
Hitting you every time you move.

As I swam through
I felt a chill
I was swimming and swimming
I wanted to get out
As I kept going to find the shore
Nothing was there, but I just kept going
Going, going.

I heard a sound!
It was a boat.
I saw it vaguely in the distance
I looked behind to see if anything was there
But there wasn't
So I started swimming as fast as I could.

But the strange thing is
When I got there, it was gone.

Olivia Halsall (12)
Dunottar School

THE SPREADING DEVASTATION

Happiness, laughter
It will never be the same.
Now the news has been broken
We all feel to blame.

No more lambs
No more goats
No more cows
No fresh milk
No sheep's coats
No more loving the farm from my heart.

It's now all gone in a swish
In a chop in a bang and a plop.
The 'bringers of death' have come to our farm.
Now our barn is empty and so are our hearts.

We feel pain
Now they are burnt in rubble and we will never
See them again.
Tears, blood, shame and blame,
But we know it will never be the same again.

Loss of money, loss of goods,
It's not only farms it's
Hotels, mountains, fields, camp sites, tourists
The general feel.

Can we start again
Or is all hope lost?
Burned, slaughtered, murdered, stolen.

Once it is over, I want to start again
Get back the happiness and laughter.
Take away the shame and blame.
I want my heart and life back
I want to feel the same.

Rachel Foreman (12)
Dunottar School

LIFE UNDER THE SEA

Water flows day and night continuously as in a rhythm.
It bashes and flows in different directions.

The sea is beautiful and calm at times,
Yet cruel and wild at other times,
Though life changes above the sea.
Who knows what happens down under?

Life under the sea can be beautiful and it can be dull.
But the animals who live down under are fascinating.

Dolphins moving and echoing,
Singing to each other
Alongside with their babies.
Starfish flowing from one direction to another,
Hunting for food as it passes along the rough sand.

Many things happen down under,
Things not everyone knows about.

So respect the sea.
It is magnificent, yet cruel.

Kelly-Ann Young Kong (12)
Dunottar School

IN THE DARK OF THE NIGHT

Fingers of mist strangled the night,
  many hours till morning light,
There's still time to scare a child,
  whilst the night is young and wild.

Not a night to walk
  across the haunted moors.
Not a time to bellow
  to the strayed four-legged fellow.

From moistened ground one step is heard,
  and magnified ten times each word.
Approaching prey of the night is born,
  for the man who magic will perform.

In a sweating palm, terror is held
  to stop it reaching his mind.
Death, cold spirits creep up his spine,
  on a windy, misty winter's time.

Fleeing into arms of evil,
  departing from the safe
Sorcerers have captured his mind,
  he'll be led on to their place.

In their place, he'll do as they please,
  until they put his mind at ease.
When a blinding light lit the darkening night.

Katie Murrell (12)
Dunottar School

QUESTIONS?

What has happened?
Who has done it?
All these questions, people asking
But what are the answers?
Is the answer to fight back?
Is there a right, is there a wrong?
Why do they keep on singing that same old song?

If I were President, I wouldn't know what to do
Would you? Or you? Or you?
When I saw it on the telly I couldn't believe it
Why would someone do that?
And here we go again, all the questions flooding in
Like an over-filling dam waiting to burst!
Why is it for violence they still have a thirst?

I suppose it makes you think
The world is not such a nice place after all.
It just makes me so cross that so many people died
Because one man believed in something.
But I think there is one good thing which has come out of this
That we, as a nation, have learned to stick
Together and be there for one another whatever
Goes on.
Perhaps one day, they will learn to sing a new song!

Lottie Faulkner (12)
Dunottar School

A HALLOWE'EN NIGHT

A rainstorm on a Hallowe'en night
A crack, a stumble
As the winds moan on.
Some beady eyes
A prowl, a peep.

The rain pattering on the leaves,
The trees swaying,
But who is in the woods?
A bear, a fox or could it be a person?

Someone grabs me from behind,
I scream like thunder
Echoing through the forest,
But no one hears my pain.

Locked in a cupboard
Trying to escape
The door slams
And I hear the pattering of shoes.
I try to reach up, but I am tied up.

But some hope in the corner,
A little axe.
I stretch my foot out and 'bingo'
Chop, chop, off comes the rope.
I open the door and run
I will never forget the feeling
I had that day.

Charlotte Allen (12)
Dunottar School

WAKEY, WAKEY!

'Wakey, wakey, rise and shine.'
'What's the time Mum, what's the time?'

'It's 6.30 you know that
Now get downstairs and feed the cat.'

Cat's done
Breakfast's ready,
'Don't rush Charlie, eat it steady.'

Had my breakfast
Getting dressed
Oh my goodness, where's my vest!

'What's the time Mum, what's the time?'

'It's nearly seven, are you dressed?
Pack your school bag you've got that test.'

School bag packed
I'm all ready
How can this satchel be so heavy?

Car is ready
We're on the road
What's this sign
Oh no! Road closed!

'What's the time Mum, what's the time?'

Charlotte Fryer (12)
Dunottar School

SEPTEMBER THE 11TH

The eleventh of September
Is the day I will always remember,
Five thousand precious lives gone,
Without a flicker of guilt,
Destroying liberty and freedom,
Upon which the stars and stripes are built.

The two tallest buildings,
Representing hope and peace,
Were demolished by ignorant terrorists,
Who didn't use words,
But used their fists.

'Good will prevail over evil,'
Was the headline from The Times.
These men are cowards
And they are feeble,
How could they have performed these terrible crimes?

They were willing to risk everything,
Just to make a point,
Their dreams, their hopes, their lives,
Selfishly not thinking of those who may die.

The depressing sight,
Reduced many to tears,
The nightmare had come true,
Which is many people's worst fears.

Satan's face rose out of the clouds,
Blazing flames engulfed the city.
The skyscrapers fell to dust,
The arsonists came from above
And yet this terrible crime,
Brought America together with trust, hope and love.

Natalie Jones (12)
Dunottar School

GET UP!

The alarm goes off at six-fifteen,
We're the laziest family you've ever seen!
Mum gets up half an hour later,
Shrieking *'Get up!'* Oh how I hate her!
I roll right over and face the wall,
With no intention to get up at all.
To my sister she bellows 'It's seven-thirty!
You must have a shower, your hair is dirty!'
There's still no movement from any child,
So then my mum gets really wild.
She stamps her feet and pleads and begs,
'Please get up you sleepyheads!'
Then Dad gets up, his hair on end,
And says, 'You drive me round the bend!'
Next thing I know it's ten to eight,
My mum is now in a terrible state!
She's running around like a headless chicken,
Threatening to give us a right good kicking!
I stumble up and crawl to the shower,
We must be at school in half an hour.
Suddenly it's ten past eight,
My sister is crying 'I can't be late!'
Mum shouts 'This has gone too far!
I'm going to go and sit in the car!'
Now I really start to worry,
Whilst my dad shouts, 'Hurry! Hurry!'
I clean my teeth and wash my face,
And pack some tissues just in case.
I shove on my shoes and walk out the door,
I shan't sleep late anymore!

Chloë Cox (12)
Dunottar School

THE WORLD, WORLD, WORLD

The world is a peaceful place,
Place, place, place

Just a rustle in the tree
Tree, tree, tree

The birds singing,
Singing, singing, singing

The rabbits come out of their burrows
Burrows, burrows, burrows

The flowers swaying
Swaying, swaying, swaying

The sun is rising,
Rising, rising, rising

The world is now coming to life,
Life, life, life.

Claire Coleman (11)
Dunottar School

THE RAINBOW

Chilled like ice
With the colours of a seven-sided dice
Shining through the night
Upon a mountain

Cool and clear
Shining like a brightly polished spear
Trickling away all fear
Like a fountain

Pots of gold
In wives tales of old
Colours that could never be told
. . . Upon a mountain

Pippa Caddick (12)
Dunottar School

THE LEGEND

(Based on the poem 'Legend')

Through the mist
Of a world far away
I seek freedom
Day by day

I shall climb every mountain
Swim every sea
I shall endure all
Until I find where I should be

I shall reach to the sky
And grab a shining star
To keep with me
Near and far.

I shall skim the clouds
Of a world up high
I shall do everything,
If I could, I would fly.

I shall reach what I want
One day or one night
And I will make sure
That I shall win this fight.

Sarah Jawad (12)
Dunottar School

THE TWIN TOWERS

The air was filled with despair,
The ground was trampled with fear,
And there was a moment of silence
Silence, silence
And there was silence and then
A bustle of talk.

The air was full of gasps,
There was a sudden jolt and a
Mark to where it had started.
People ran, people jumped and screamed
Screaming, screaming
And there were people screeching until it was done.

There were papers flying into the air,
There were bodies lying on the ground and
People were caring.
There were people crying thinking it was
Not fair.
Fair, fair!
And people thinking it was not fair.

One hour later there was a huge loud rumble,
The people were mumbling, thinking it was lumbering
One by one the towers began to crumble
Crumble, crumble!
There was a crumble and many screams.

Leandra Kastell (11)
Dunottar School

BAY

The whisking of her tail
The drumming of her feet,
I'll bet she could almost jump a thousand feet!
The feel of creaking leather,
The smell of sweat and grass,
It makes you almost feel like you can touch the stars.
Her fur a dazzling bay,
Her mane a shining glow.
All you have to do is crack the whip and go,
The way she always galloped
Across the fields and away,
It made the world just disappear
On that lovely hot spring day.

Emily Barker (12)
Dunottar School

A LONELY TREE IN A DARK WOOD

A lonely tree burning in a dark wood
The bright red flickering flames
dancing from branch to branch
lighting up the night sky.
The crackling and crunching of the leaves
falling softly to the ground.
The withering dying tree, swaying in the cold wind.
The thick smoke fills the wood,
The warm glowing embers
are all that are left of
a lonely tree in a dark wood.

Rebecca Warrender (14)
Hawley Place School

WHAT DO YOU SEE?

What do you see midwife? What do you see?
What are you thinking, when you look at me?
A tiny baby with far-away eyes
Whose mother sleeps quietly, right by her side.

What do you see mother? What do you see?
What are you thinking, when you're looking at me?
A small lonely child, who is but three
Who plays all alone, quite happily.

What do you see teachers? What do you see?
What are you thinking, when you're looking at me?
A shy quiet student, who never replies,
But always looks deeply into your eyes.

What do you see students? What do you see?
What are you thinking, when you're looking at me?
A weird little loner, who sits all on her own,
In a huge round bubble, she's always alone.

What do you see colleagues? What do you see?
What are you thinking, when you're looking at me?
A silent young worker, in her office alone,
Who's even too scared, to answer the phone.

What do you see vicar, What do you see?
What are you thinking, when you're looking at me?
An insensitive daughter, whose mother has died,
And when she found out, she never even cried.

What do you see carers? What do you see?
What are you thinking, when you're looking at me?
A haggard old woman, all tattered and torn
Who can't even remember the date she was born.

What do you see nurses? What do you see?
What are you thinking, when you're looking at me?
A wrinkled up woman, who dribbles her food
And you just point, laughing. I find it so rude!

So what do you see people? What do you see?
What exactly are you thinking, when you're looking at me?
A one hour old baby? A three year old child?
A student? A colleague?
A mother so mild?
A senile old woman, lying on her bed?
Not scared to be alone
Not scared to be dead.

Joanna Cagney (13)
Hawley Place School

THE MUGGER

One drop of sweat
upon my fearful brow.
Eyes looking in all directions,
body ready and waiting
for one slight movement.
A chase for my sincerity!
A feeling of regret runs
swiftly down my spine.
As I run towards her
and take her purse.

Felicity Bagley (15)
Hawley Place School

A Voice Not Worth Listening To!

A rattle
A teddy bear
A small rocking chair
A bottle
A nappy
A tantrum, here or there.
This is a baby with its whole life ahead,
Not having to worry about what time to go to bed.

A pen
A desk
A large double bed
A mobile
A boyfriend
Lots of things inside her head.
That is a teenager with a happy frame of mind,
Not having to think about a job or home to find.

A career
A husband
A car with five gears.
A home
Work colleagues
A voice inside her ears.
This is an adult with nothing to fear
A roof over her head and no time to shed a tear.

A gun
4 lives
Her leader wants much more.
A bomb
200 lives
Now she really has the score.
This mindless adult listened to the voice inside her head.
Now she's a terrorist with 204 people dead.

Anisha Trivedy (13)
Hawley Place School

THE WORLD GRIEVES

The waves come lapping on the shore
The rain comes blowing from the sky
The people go about their day
A tear falls slowly from an eye

The moon keeps grinning through the clouds
The leaves are falling from the trees
Money keeps on being made
And honey by the bumblebees

A deadly silence, the people grieve
The world stops turning round and round
Animals stay inside their burrows
Death is not a pleasant sound.

Siân Stephens (13)
Hawley Place School

THE LETTER

Dear Mum,

I don't know how to say this
So I'll just say it from the heart,
This is so hard for me
I don't know where to start.

From the moment he walks in the door
To the moment he walks out,
There's broken glass all over the floor
It's like all he does is shout.

The countless nights I've spent restlessly
Thinking about what I should do.
I was going to do it there and then Mum
The only thing stopping me, was you.

I can hear thuds downstairs now
The baby starts crying
I'm going to do it tonight Mum
I'm not afraid of dying

I hear him storm out
And you hush the baby.
I wonder what he's done this time?
Broken your nose again, maybe?

I'm going to go downstairs now
And see if you're all right,
And then I'll go to bed
And wish you a goodnight.

And in the morning, read this letter
I'll be holding it in my hand,
Know why I did it mum
Please try to understand.

I love you more than anything
I'll miss you now and forever,
I don't want to see you hurt Mum.
Not now, not then, not ever.

Natasha Marsh (15)
Hawley Place School

MANHATTAN

The morning had started like any other day,
Some people at work, others on their way.
Yet not three hours since the sun did rise,
Something had happened that blackened the skies.
By almost nine o'clock the first jet had hit,
And one of the towers had started to split.
As if that had not caused enough pain
A few minutes later one struck again.
And when the Center was hit with another blow,
The after-effects were far but slow.

But much worse things did happen that day,
As we later discovered to our dismay,
That thousands of men worked in each of the towers,
And finding survivors could take hours.
So just how many men did die that day
Whilst going along on their innocent way?
The final toll may never be known
As still no more survivors are to be shown!
But what is far more daunting than this
Is how men can sink into such an abyss.
That they could be too wicked to care,
At the destruction below as New York was laid bare!

Emma Dodd (13)
Hawley Place School

MY PLACE!

When I am on stage
I am like a coin which has disappeared behind the sofa cushion.
I am lost in a never-ending world of peace,
I drown in the music and melt into a puddle on the floor.

It is darkness until I step into the light,
I look out to be blinded by the glimmering spectacles
But I don't care; I am alone and in my world,
It is my time, my place, my world.

When I hear the music begin,
I feel the fireworks being lit.
Ready for an explosion to run through my body
And burst out through my head.

I am firing through everyone's body
My spirit jumps from inside me, and bounces off the walls.
The electricity runs through my veins,
As I tremble with weakness, yet with fire in my heart,
And a passion to carry on
Before it's over!

The music stops
I stop.
The world stops
I stop!

Carly Meyers (13)
Hawley Place School

THE GIRAFFE

As she elegantly ambles
Across the scorching dusty plain,
In all her dignity,
Her calf frolics and gambles
Like a baby lamb,
And is protected by its mother
From unpleasant foe.

With her strong rope of a tail,
She sways and swishes it,
To scare the flies and ticks.

She stretches her tall laddered
Elongated neck,
And nibbles from a tree,
Her long snake-like tongue
Savouring its flavours.

Her soft cool limpid eyes
Are alert and attentive.

She then rests peacefully,
Whilst her brown islands
Are dappled in the
Bright sun's rays
Amongst the
Green emerald
Trees.

Freya Gigg (13)
Hawley Place School

I AM HERE AND YOU ARE THERE!

I see the face looking at me,
I can feel his breath on my back
And as he walks towards me
I can feel his feet tapping,
Tapping, tapping - he is getting nearer.

Bang! A bullet went right into my back.
I can still feel it now
Now that I am gone.
I still feel the blood gushing out of the wound.
I fell with a bump and another shot was fired.

I saw a white light
I could hear someone calling me.
Should I have? Shouldn't I have?
I did, it felt like . . . well I'm not going to tell you!
I can see everyone; I even watched my funeral.

Now do you see? Don't be scared, I'm here and you're there!
Waiting for you to come.
The one thing you can depend on is that some day,
Maybe tomorrow, maybe next week or for a few years
You will be here, dead with me.

Sarah Halligan (14)
Hawley Place School

THE SKELETON

The last leaves float to the ground
And whistle to the end of the path,
The tree is left bare
Alone, sad and gloomy
It twists and turns
Its long bony fingers wither,
But still trying to reach the sky.

All of a sudden it shrinks
Giving out an enormous shriek.
It twists and turns to the ground,
With it, its roots decay
The wind subsides,
The skeleton dies
And all that's left is silence.

Charlotte Harwood (14)
Hawley Place School

HELPLESS

As I stood there
Just watching,
Thinking that I couldn't
Do anything.
Then I heard a cry
Above me,
There was a young girl
Screaming out of a window.
Screaming at me
So that I could see
She was going to die.
I was probably her last
Chance of help.
But did I help her?
No!
I couldn't
Or wouldn't.
Why waste my life?
Mine's fine how it is!
Or is it
Now!?

Rebecca Pratap (13)
Hawley Place School

WHAT WE HAVE BECOME

The same voice filters through the receiver
But the sound seems different somehow,
You hold your ground and firm beliefs,
I cannot change them, I should know by now.

The image I know doesn't fit the voice,
Confusion builds up with the tears,
I wait for the blunt words I am expecting
To confirm my worst fears.

Churning around in my head are the memories,
Of holding, of caring, of loving, of needing.
In your head memories are more likely to be
Of fighting, of crying, of bitterness, of teasing.

I care too much for you to see
Or hear from my voice obviously.
I offer my hand in a last desperate attempt
You just push it away, viciously.

You say the second chance has gone,
With the third and fourth, for both of us.
As I look back to old words silently,
I recall them to imply *'just lust'*.

Inside, the gap that you have left,
Is ripped at by vicious goodbyes
And accusations that have never been true.
We remember our time as a lie.

The same voice filters through the receiver,
But the sound seems different somehow.
As you bite out the words to say goodbye,
You won't be back. I should know by now.

Kate Maskell (16)
John Ruskin College

I'VE TRIED

I've always tried to see her
the way she sees herself,
I've tried to find the truth - but what does it mean to her?
Something seems to be missing,
No will to move on, or look back
We cannot change the past

I've tried to understand her
the way she does herself,
I've tried to uncover her sadness and why she never smiles
Sitting, sad and lonely
that's all she ever does.
I cannot comprehend it
the strain is far too much

I'm still trying to hold her
the way she did with me
Trying to stand and wait for her
Longing to release a fantasy
of a mind-filled madness
where dreams are made to come true

However,

I'm trying to be truthful
the way she taught me to be
Trying to unravel false words
wrapped around confusion.

I'll leave a rope for her to climb
but I cannot make her climb it
I'll still stand and wait for her
And I'll never turn away.

Samantha Jane Rowle (16)
John Ruskin College

ETERNAL BUTTERFLY

I am but a butterfly
Clasped in the hands of time
Longing for the immunity of human life,
Wanting the power to be the predator.

I live a life of anguish,
Of worry and fear and hate,
A life of longing
Longing for the end.

For I am not just a mere butterfly
I can never live and die.
Because immortality is a curse that
I have brought upon myself,
A curse that will always be alive.

I am but a butterfly
Clasped in the hands of time

Forever.

Kayley McMorrow (16)
John Ruskin College

MY PET

Her heart is warmer than
Summer nights
Her eyes twinkle brighter
Than the brightest lights.

Her fur is soft like
Spider silk,
Her nose is cold and wet
Like milk.

She wags her tail every day
She is full of energy
And bursting to play.

There is nothing to change
Nothing to mend,
All I can say is that
She is my best friend.

Charlotte Howe (11)
St Teresa's School, Dorking

MY PET HAMSTER

There is a fluffy thing in a bedroom window
It is grey and white, it has fluffy feet.
Is it a hamster. It must be?
It's small and looks like a mouse.

It looks so cute, it has
A fluffy tail and a fluffy body.
Its heart is red with a pumping speed
And it has eyes from Heaven.

It has soft feet like a scarf,
It has eyes that glow
Like the moonlight.
It has lips that are silky
Like nails from a human.

It eats so much, its cheeks
Look like muffins packed together.
It has feet, a nose, eyes, ears and a mouth
And it has a special love inside him
Just for you.

Melissa Oldridge (11)
St Teresa's School, Dorking

RUDI

This little dog of mine
Really is quite funny.
Brown and white, piebald
He is best of all.

Rudi likes to play outside,
Especially when it's sunny.
He gets the wind in his tail
Then he is rather funny.

He really can be quite a rebel,
And oh, so bad!
He tears up the garden
That makes mum mad!

There's a mongrel who lives nearby
Of some, he is quite jealous.
He chases her endlessly,
He can be quite zealous.

As evening falls
And mealtime calls
My little friend becomes quite greedy,
He smells his food and boy, he's speedy.

Amanda Morrison (11)
St Teresa's School, Dorking

FRIENDS

Written with a pen, sealed with a kiss,
You are my friend let's live in bliss,
You told me this the other day
Let me tell you this today
You've been my friend since I was two
I'll always be here for you.

I know we've both had our troubles,
But I pray I'll be there on the double.
Even though you're leaving here
I'll always have a listening ear.
I'll never forget your loving smile
If you feel lonely just pick up and dial.

Rachel Laws (13)
St Teresa's School, Dorking

PLANET EARTH

The world wakes
The sun rolls through the sky
Lighting the darkness
Night has left behind.

The day breaks
People start to sigh
Another day of work
Emotions running high.

The day is ending
People choose to allay
Bringing to a close
The story of today.

The world rests
The sun goes to hide,
It's time for the moon to rise
In the setting sky.

The day has gone
Nothing can be changed,
Until tomorrow
When we can start again.

Carina Crouch (13)
St Teresa's School, Dorking

JOURNEY

I set sail with my pretty black cat
We set sail like the night bat,
We were as happy as could be
We didn't have a care in the world.

I said 'Stay with me with glee. Black cat
Of my heart. Will you please?'
She turned to me and her eyes twinkled
She had that sort of look 'Yes, forever in my heart.'

I looked into the crystal water of the sea
It seemed so quiet and calm, just the place
So we caught fish for tea.
After that, we went for a swim in the sea.

The next day we went to an island
There we stayed for some time.
One day I awoke to find the cat and boat had gone,
I saw my cat go, but never to come back
So my heart was broken.

Ayana Ollerhead (11)
St Teresa's School, Dorking

THE FISH

The water blue light shines on the fishes tail
As he travels his path without a wail
He is going to see Coddy his fishy friend
Who lives down the river, around the bend.

He has seen Coddy, his teeth gleaming white
He is mowing his seaweed without a fright
'Hey Coddy!' He calls 'How are you?'
'I'm all right Fishy. How about you?'

As he moved on from Coddy he saw a big worm
But he was not hungry
It looked so so plump, he gave it a go
But it wouldn't come off!
Quick, he'd better make haste,
And soon he'll be out of this place.

Our dear little Fishy as you may have guessed
Ended up as the Jones' meal
For their next dinner guest!

Harriet McAtee (11)
St Teresa's School, Dorking

NEW BEGINNING

I wake up in the sunlight
Feeling cheerful, happy and bright
I wipe the sleep out of my eyes
That's usually all it takes

It brings me back to my senses
Fear, anxiety, my whole body tenses
This is the existence, which I call my life
What is the point of calling it my life?

It is not a life it is just an endless amount of fears
The thought of that day brings to my eyes tears
The pain, the suffering, the woe
I vow to myself one day I'll let it all go.

Now the day has come to let go of my sorrow
No, not later, not tomorrow
Yes, this a fight worth winning
I know, I know it's time for a new beginning.

Amaka Ubah (13)
St Teresa's School, Dorking

LIFE

Life can be difficult
Life can be suffering
Life can be depressive
Life is a journey of hardness

Life can be merry
Life can be kindness
Life can be happiness
Life can be a journey of freedom

Life can be fun
Life can be dull
Life can be dangerous
Life is a journey of obstacles

Life can be boyfriends
Life can be engagements
Life can be marriage
Life is a journey of love

No one knows life
No one knows 'after life'
No one knows your future
All we know is that life is
A journey uphill or downhill.

Anna Hartley (11)
St Teresa's School, Dorking

THE ZODIAC

I look into the sky above,
the dark rich colours swirling round.
Stars, small but bright, as they sparkle in the velvet sky,
the stars making patterns, the shapes of the zodiac.
Having had a look, after a while I begin to see.

I see Leo, the lion, standing proud amongst the rest.
Though I look for a long time
I can't see the rest.
But then soon the light starts to take over,
and the characters of the zodiac are gone.

Alice Prentice (11)
St Teresa's School, Dorking

WINTER IS HERE

The sun is falling lower each day
Autumn is going, winter is coming.
The sky is getting dark
The dogs start to bark.

As snow falls slowly
The ponds start to freeze
The cars are getting frosty
And then comes the cold breeze.

Out comes the snowdrops
Sprouting here and there
Then out hops the robin
Bobbing here and there.

Christmas Day is near now
The shops are getting busy
People wearing heavy warm coats
Buying little toy boats.

Hip, hip hooray, it's Christmas Day
Oh what fun and glory
Lots of gifts from people you love
Can you see the white dove?

Harriet Lewin (11)
St Teresa's School, Dorking

GUARDIANS OF THE EARTH

Reaching into eternity;
a wide, empty space,
it floods the heavens.
A beautiful blue,
dark and immense
filling the air above.
Sky, you fill the world.

A cold light;
the moon rises.
White, glowing,
shining with pureness;
the essence of beauty.
Why are you here moon?
So that the sea can follow
in my footsteps.
I am the guardian of the Earth.

Stars appear,
tingling with brightness;
as the signs of the zodiac
take shape.
Why are you here stars?
We are God's tears,
Lords of the sky
Crying, as you destroy His world.

Xenia Elsaesser (13)
St Teresa's School, Dorking

TREES IN AUTUMN

'I'm losing my hair'
Scream the others
'I'm not'
I whisper

I listen to the gales
As they whistle in my ears,
They tear at my hair
But never will they win.

The snow settles
On my arms,
Deers tear at me
Rabbits huddle
Beneath me.

Moles tunnel
Worms slide.
The wings of the birds are back
Two dozen settle on my arms.

'Hooray'
We shout and
Spring is back.

'By the way I'm a tree.'
I shout.

Elizabeth Hartley (11)
St Teresa's School, Dorking

POWERFUL GLOW

I sit upon a hilltop
Alone, quiet and still
The sun is waking from its endless slumber
It shines a powerful glow

Hiding like a small child
Behind the clouds it goes
Its rays split as it bursts through the cushioned clouds

I feel its burning heat
At the hottest part of day
The radiance from its shine
Lights up my whole face
The animals run for cover
My throat is dry and sore
But my dreams of cool water
Fill me with hope

The sun is slowly falling
Like a leaf onto the ground
The cool breeze
A wonderful feeling
A clear blue sky

The wonderful quilt of colours
Keeps me in a trance
The sun has almost gone
And I must follow his path
As the moon appears
The sun has gone
And I must go.

Rebecca Scarrott (13)
St Teresa's School, Dorking

LIFE

From the day you are born
From the day you open your eyes
Ahead of you a path so long
Yet a path so true.

I wander, day and night
In neither storm, rain or shine,
But I stand in some fog
In the corner of my mind.

I am reaching out for something
Stepping to and fro
But nothing to my liking comes
Or so my mind tells me so.

First I see a ladder
Then I see some stairs
Then a long winding path
Set foot on it I dare!

Along this everlasting path
Forever giving up all hope
They come in twos, threes and fours
Too many choices, too many doors!

As soon as I saw a twinkle
A glimmer of a star.
I said I'm going to stay here
Now I've got this far.

So on a boat I travel
Far over the sea
To the stunning horizon
Where I'll forever be!

Hannah McCulloch (11)
St Teresa's School, Dorking

MOVING ON

The early morning dew
A softly settled white sheet
Lies gently on the fields.
Dawn's companions leave footprints as they pass
Like imprints in the clouds.
For some, the day is almost over
But other closed eyes lie quietly in bed
Ready to move on with the day.

The evening frosts bite deep
Seaming barren fields
In an arctic wasteland
Burrowing creatures busily shunting,
Earthworks shifting upwards.
For some, the day has just begun
But other closed eyes lie quietly in bed
Ready to forget the day and move on.

Meggan Ireland (13)
St Teresa's School, Dorking

STARRY SKY

I am lying on the grass looking up into
the night sky.
All these different stars are looking back at me,
grinning and waving.
Some are very bright and big,
some little and faint.
Wait! What is that light shooting across the sky?
It's so quiet but yet so fast.
What can it be?
Oh of course, a shooting star!

Alexandra Lamport (11)
St Teresa's School, Dorking

RAINBOWS

The rain has stopped, I look outside,
I see a glistening sight with my eyes.
It's a rainbow! That's what I see!
Those beautiful colours that stand in front of me.
I wonder what it is like to be inside a rainbow?
I never ever tried, so I guess I will go
I take a step, it moves away.
I don't know what is wrong, it might be afraid.
I try again, this time it isn't scared.
I walk closer and closer, and then I'm there.
What should I do? Should I step inside?
So I take a large giant step inside
I shut my eyes.
I open them now, I see the sight,
It looks as beautiful as ever,
Something I don't think I am able to write.
The violet, the yellow
The green and blue
All around me.
I feel a lift from my shoe.
The rainbow is taking me somewhere.
But all I am able to do is stand and stare.
What is happening? What can I do?
The rainbow might be taking me to Timbuktu
It's now landing . . . where am I?
I'm home, so now I'll just say goodbye!

Vanessa Vanselow (11)
St Teresa's School, Dorking

MY NAUGHTY LITTLE BROTHER

My little brother is a small little thing
With the most cheekiest grin,
He is naughty constantly
Funny? Never!
Moans about everything, even the weather.
Runs around
Never stopping,
In kitchen or in the hall
Won't stop winding people up the wall.
People think that his twin brother is Dennis The Menace.
Getting into trouble all the time,
But he is your brother so you might as well
Luv him!

Fredrique Rickerd (11)
St Teresa's School, Dorking

WHERE I COME FROM

Where I come from it is
strange and blue
Not like here where it's yellow, red
and purple too
I can't believe this planet it's strange
in its shape
Not like my planet which is wibble, wobble
like jelly on a plate.
The clothes are green and thin, not like here
where they're all woven in.
On my planet the glop moves under your
feet, not like here
where it's hard and neat!

Charlotte Liparoto (11)
St Teresa's School, Dorking

My Room

It is where I go whether I feel good or bad,
It is where I go whether I feel happy or sad.
It is what awaits me when I come home
And it is where I go when I'm alone.
It is my own private space
Which you can't ever replace.
Everything in there represents my personality,
Everything in there is special to me.
In this place I can do what I want to do,
This place has no name
It's just my room.

Amber van der Graaf (13)
St Teresa's School, Dorking

Aliens

Is there life in outer space?
Are there others, not part of the human race?
Are aliens going to invade our planet?
If they do, then we've all had it!
Are they green with massive eyes?
And do they ever eat pork pies?
Or are they pink with purple spots?
And is their planet cold or hot?
What sort of language do they speak?
And are they strong or are they weak?
Is there really life on Mars?
But personally, I think I'll stick to the chocolate bars!

Bobbie Hyams (11)
The Ashcombe School

JOURNEY INTO SPACE

As I hurtled up into a midnight sky,
Watching stars pass me by,
I entered a world of incredible light,
And left behind the moonless night.

One million shimmering, brilliant specks,
Made a beautiful, wonderful, amazing effect.
Nine spectacular balls of colour,
Spinning, twisting, encircling each other.

But the gem of all this luminous display,
Cast out its burning, flickering rays.
The powerful ruler up on high,
Throwing golden beams across the sky.

Up in the world of incredible light,
I gazed down upon the moonless night,
And as I watched stars pass me by,
I plummeted down into a midnight sky.

Rachel Barker (11)
The Ashcombe School

HEART OF FIRE

Roaring like a lion,
Swirling like the sea.
The heart of fire,
Flickers ferociously.

And with a blaze of light,
The fire rises in the air.
Spreading with many colours,
Into the dark of night as if to share.

Yellow, orange and red,
To show its desire.
As the wind whispers,
'Heart of fire!'

Ruth Milne (11)
The Ashcombe School

SUN

As a ball of fire
I speed through the murky depths of the universe
All consuming darkness broken by my rays of light,
like swords, piercing a huge, dark blanket.
Stars like shining emeralds
shimmer and glint in my light.

Red-hot as I burn on,
I gaze at sphere-like planets,
Like mere dots,
the galaxy being a huge picture.

The whole world in perfect naiveté
as the sands of time slip through the fingers of men.

Men and women alike are cut down like wheat
To be born again.
Strong.
Far below I see the Earth,
Pebbles lie, untidily strewn on the beaches far below,
As the waves curl like towering mutants of the deep,
Issuing forth from the murky depths of the unknown.

Cities fall and decay into ashes
but time still looks on with perfect indifference.

Harry McEntire (11)
The Ashcombe School

GOLDEN TICKET TO HEAVEN

The blood-red, luminous mass in the sky,
A distant battlefield,
God of war.

The ear-piercing sounds of metal swords clanking,
The taste of warm, metallic blood from wounds,
The smell of the dusty red floor aggravating my hay fever,
I could feel the warm breeze coming in from the far east,
I looked up at the never-ending black hole,
The stars glimmered like jewels out of a treasure box.

A dark, clammy mist settled throughout the bloody battlefield,
A storm silently slithered into eyesight,
Red dust whirled and swirled,
The soldiers came to a halt.

Everything grew silent and a dark, black merciless cloud
Hung over the battlefield as if it were bringing bad news,
The wind whispered furiously,
As if it had some locked-up secret urging to be let out.

Volcanic lava spewed, spluttered and sizzled out of the dusty floor,
As if it were choking violently,
The ground shook with anticipation,
Anticipation to kill noble soldiers,
Who brought on this death quest?
So many innocent killed,
Death, such an awful price to pay,
Death slips from your fingers like sand being blown by wind.

This wasn't any old war,
This was a war to kill evil,
And the prize was a golden ticket to Heaven.

Why should the evil have a golden ticket to Heaven?
Life's unfair,
And full of locked-up secrets you can never unfold.

Holly Gowers (14)
The Ashcombe School

A GOLDEN CHILD

As a silent explosion fills the air,
A sudden spurt of happiness grows once more,
A new book is made,
A new cell is combined,
A new black hole turns in,
A baby is born.
It's not any baby though
The Golden baby grows in size,
but as it grows, so does happiness.
They are in every soul,
fighting to get out, to bring even more joy.
Golden babies evolve into Golden children,
as that happens, happiness turns into friendship.
Nobody has ever seen a Golden child,
but you know they're there,
you can feel it in every set of eyes.

Christopher Harnan (11)
The Ashcombe School

SEASONS IN THE RING

Winter has the advantage as the fight begins,
With his frosty attitude and nippy defence,
His cool approach shows he knows he will win,
He's thrown autumn right into the fence!

Autumn surrenders and spring steps in,
She leaps into the ring ready for anything,
Winter's beginning to tire after a blow to his shin,
He's dripping with embarrassment as he exits the ring.

Summer's tagged and in she runs,
She's bursting with bright, clever tactics,
Spring's no match for summer's strong punch,
I think spring needs a bit more practice.

Autumn's ready to go again,
Summer realises she's no longer so hot,
Summer's clear skies subside into rain,
And she's cornered in a tight spot.

Join us again next year for the seasons in the ring.

Just have some fun it's free for all,
Same competitors - different bout,
We're all spectators so enjoy it all,
We'll be back for more, no doubt!

Eve Collyer Merritt (11)
The Ashcombe School

IN THE NIGHT SKY

Stars twinkling clear and bright
In the midnight sky
A whole other world up there
Waiting to be explored
How I wish to go there

Way up high
Pitch-black sky
Plunging into outer space
I will go to that place
Some day . . .

Elaine Wolvey (11)
The Ashcombe School

MYSTIC MEG'S HOROSCOPES

Welcome, my friends, to the house of fortune,
Horoscopes by Mystic Meg,
Tell me your star signs my dears,
Librans, watch out for your leg!

Aries will get a pay rise,
Taurus, mind you don't fall.
Aquarius will go swimming,
And give Pisces a call.

Virgo will win a beauty contest,
But everyone will agree,
That Capricorn should have won,
Go on; try it, you will see.

Gemini will get in a fight,
Leo will lose a bet,
Cancer will shoot sideways,
When Scorpio is met.

Sagittarius will go on holiday.
And maybe never return,
Now go my friends and rest awhile,
As I watch my fire burn.

Megan Louise Davis (11)
The Warwick School

THE ZODIAC

What is in the stars above?
Do they tell fate and predict love?
Can constellations really see?
What happens through eternity?

Twelve star signs known around the Earth,
Showing us of what we're worth,
Symbols and signs telling us what,
What happens and what will not.

Aquarius are just and loyal,
Libra's unafraid of toil,
Scorpio's are passionate but beware the sting,
Sagittarius see everything.

Cancers protect and see you through,
Leo is always there for you,
Virgo's are kind and always sharing,
Pisces are forever caring.

Capricorn's are patient and take their time,
Taurus never step out of line,
Gemini can convince you the moon is the sun,
Aries bring joy, happiness and fun.

The twelve signs shine among the stars,
Telling us just who we are,
And you know as each day is nigh,
The zodiac doesn't lie.

Ruth Allen (14)
The Warwick School

THE ZODIAC

Who is youthful, witty
Persuasive and pretty,
And their sign is that of the twins?
And the kind and sensitive,
Helpful, supportive
Animal has gills and fins.
The goat's practical and patient,
Archers fun and intelligent,
Which one will do anything to win?
The lion is loving,
Faithful and encouraging.
And will help you to find your dreams.
The scales are calming,
Laid back and charming,
Can argue for anything it seems.
Who is passionate and forceful,
Can easily enthral you,
But can have a poisonous sting?
Cancer's shrewd and protective,
The bull is sensitive,
All of them able to win.
Loyal and honest,
Perspective and modest,
Aquarians are really quite bright
Dynamic and fun,
As bright as the sun,
Arians are always right
So here are the stars
They'll say if you will go far,
Will they discover your plight?

Cayleigh Spooner (14)
The Warwick School

THE DAY I WILL NEVER FORGET

An ordinary day, an ordinary morning.
A woke up tired, sleepy and yawning.
Dragged myself downstairs, sat down,
Grabbed the paper and forced away my frown.
Turned to my horoscope, page sixty-six.
Started to read, my eyes fixed.
'You will meet old family and friends.
Smile the day away and hang on till the end,
Then all your pain will fade away,
Happier will you feel at the dawning of a day.'
So I smiled the day away, smiled through the pain,
Smiled even when my heart played up again.
Then midnight came, the stars aligned.
Thoughts kept racing through my mind.
There they stood, just like the stars had said.
Looking like they had never left.
Blood, flesh, mind and heart
My pain was over at long last.
Finally I could see my family in Heaven,
Over were those painful years of seven.
Then all of my family received a hug from me,
And I follow them to where I would spend eternity.

Jennifer Wallace (14)
The Warwick School

ZODIAC

Leo the lion, as strong as an ox,
Leo the lion, as cunning as a fox
Leo the lion, as brave as can be
Leo the lion, perhaps that's you, but it's definitely me!

The stars shine out bright in the velvet, black sky
I wonder how Leo the lion can fly?
Fortune telling horoscopes they're all the same
But many people play the destiny game.

Dhanesh Patel (11)
The Warwick School

THE ZODIAC

Zodiac is the star signs, high up in the sky
Why are they there? We don't know why.
Aquarius is the water carrier, fetching water
Pisces is the fish, eternally swimming.
Whilst Aries the ram, is strong and mighty
These are the signs for winter when cold rules supreme.
Spring starts and with the sun bold Taurus comes out
Taurus the bull, the strongest of all
Then Gemini the twins, who are kind and helpful
But Cancer the crab, is slick and fast
Bringing summer to an end, then
The autumn begins.
Leo the lion, monumentally rules all the sky
With Virgo the maid, the girl who loves all
Libra is the cleverest, weighing all in his scales
Autumn ends and winter is near.
Scorpio the scorpion is very small yet has the capacity to harm all
Sagittarius rules mankind
He's quick as a horse with the mind of a man.
Capricorn the goat is the last on parade
And lives on the Earth that we have made
The cycle restarts and winter returns.

Matthew Frawley (11)
The Warwick School

ZODIAC

What's in store for me today?
Miss my train?
Go insane?
Get stuck in a lift?
Fall off a cliff?
Trip down the stairs?
Chased by bears?
Get in a fight?
Miss my flight?
Win the lottery?
break my crockery?
Better read my horoscopes!

Maybe . . .
Catch a dove?
Fall in love?
Miss a step?
Get all wet?
Break my pen?
Fall off Big Ben?
Stub my toe?
Feel real low?
Caught in the rain?
What a pain!
Better read my horoscopes!

Or . . .
Slip on ice?
Find some mice?
Catch a bee?
Drink some tea?
Borrow a book?
Attempt to cook?
Wear a skirt?
Be a huge flirt?
Eat a kebab?
Hire a cab?
Better read my horoscopes!

Lucy Cornwell (14)
The Warwick School

ZODIAC AND CONSTELLATIONS

Cancer the Crab is in the sky,
At midnight in July,
Roaming the clouds,
he must be very proud.
Aquarius carrying water in a jar,
Swimming by, walking far,
Making Constellations,
And giving peace to the nations.
All in the dark sky,
At midnight in July.

Adam Bauldry (11)
The Warwick School

CONSTELLATIONS

Stars in the sky
High, high, high.
Little Bear in the air
Where, where, where?
Pegasus flying high
Flying through the silent night sky.

Where's Cancer the crab, in the sky
Watching the people walk on by.
Leo the lion, high up in space
Watching the world just in case.
See the bull Taurus, walk in the sky
When we see him, we ask him why.

Scorpio lies in the stars
Looking over Pluto and Mars.
Great Bear in the air
Watching over Little Bear
Stars in the sky
High, high, high.

Andrea Bent (10)
The Warwick School

ZODIAC

Can I tell what you're like by the day you were born?
Just by the moon and the stars,
Whether you're Aquarius or Capricorn?
Are girls from Venus and boys from Mars?

Can you really be defined by a date,
Libra Pisces and Scorpio,
Does it really say what you love and hate
Gemini, Taurus and Leo.

Is everyone born between the 21st of March
And the 20th of April the same?
Fun-loving and dynamic.
Is it all a game
Is every Aries quick?

Can you really be defined by a date?
Capricorn, Aries and Aquarius,
Does it really say what you love and hate,
Cancer, Virgo and Sagittarius.

Deborah Pearse (14)
The Warwick School

ZODIAC

The practical Capricorn, patient and clever
Intellectual Sagittarius boring never
Passionate Scorpio forceful with a sting
Charming Libra can talk their way out of anything
Diligent Virgo shy and exact
Faithful Leo, full of love and tact
Protective Cancer who is always in the know
Youthful Gemini a friend not a foe
Placid Taurus a head like a bull
Confident Aries quick to catch your fall
Sensitive Pisces helpful and kind
Honest Aquarius with no lies in mind
This is the Zodiac
The stars in the sky
Day to day predictions of your life floating by
Close to your heart
In touch with your mind
The Zodiac predictions
Seek and you shall find.

Lucy Moon (15)
The Warwick School

SUPERSTITIOUS STUART'S STAR SIGNS

What is your star sign sir?
Is it Pisces or Taurus?
Do you even have a star sign?
Tell me is it Taurus?
Tell me your star sign please, sir
You could be extremely rich!

Can I see your palm, sir?
Have you got a long life line?
Please let me see, sir!
Or is it a short line?
Please, please, please, sir!

Will you look into my crystal ball, sir?
Into the wispy, white smoke?
I can see a face, sir!
He's quite a handsome bloke!
Look, he's got a moustache sir!
He kind of looks like you!

Will you look at the sky, sir?
Can you see Sagittarius?
Can you see Fornax sir?
Can you see Aquarius?
Look, there's Hydra sir!
Can you see Capricornus?

Soon there will be a love in your life sir!
She could be from anywhere!
You might meet her in a pub sir!
She might give you a scare!

You might meet her on the dance floor, sir!
She might have purple, spiky hair!
Only I know what your future holds!

Stuart Burrows (11)
The Warwick School

ZODIAC

Aries the ram with his fiery eyes,
Never as calm as the great, blue skies.

Taurus the bull's between April and May,
He orders you around till the end of the day.

Gemini has two faces,
They have different worlds and live in ridiculous places.

You may not have heard of the spider
Because he hangs from the sky
His sign falls between June and July.

Cancer's the crab he'll pinch you hard,
He'll soon say sorry and give you a card.

Leo the lion, roars so loud,
He stands tall, strong and very proud.

Virgo dwells in forest and in woods
She always carries expensive goods.

Libra the scales has perfect balance,
He can do lots and has many talents.

Scorpio the scorpion has a piercing tail,
He makes you scream and he makes you wail.

Sagittarius is half man, half horse,
He shoots many arrows with tremendous force.

Capricorn - that's me!

Aquarius carries liquids so clear,
And looks after children he holds so dear.

Pisces the fish, last but not least,
He is a wonderful, scaly beast.

Francesca Hoyle (11)
The Warwick School

ZODIAC

Can we read our fate into the shining
Stars we see at night?
Is it true, what they say,
Or is it short of sight?

I'm an Aquarius, you see,
I'm honest, loyal and true
But if you're the same sign as me,
Is it true for you?

If Sagittarius, are you smart?
Are Capricorns, the planners?
If Leo, are you big of heart?
Can Cancer forget their manners?

If Scorpio, can you sting?
Gemini and Aries, fun?
Libra talk out of anything?
Taurus help anyone?

Are Pisces really very sweet?
Are Virgo shy, are Virgo neat?
But for our signs, we can still see
The differences of you and me.

Some say that all are full of love
That's locked up in your heart
The keys to some hearts is a friend,
Some keys lie in the stars.

And as I watch the stars go by,
Up in the Milky Way
I think I love to see the stars,
I think so every day.

Monique Davis (14)
The Warwick School

ZODIAC COLOURS

Yellow for stubborn Aries the ram.
Strong, vibrant colours for arrogant Leo
Fiery like Sagittarius.
Lively Aquarius.
Intellectual Gemini.
Idealistic and calm Libra
Stubborn like Taurus the bull
Dominant Capricorn
Careful like Virgo
Secretive Pisces, blue is the choice of this fish
Kind Cancer, green is the colour for this crab.
Emotional like Scorpio.

Daniella McCarthy (11)
The Warwick School

ZODIAC

Inside the darkness,
The plain black box,
Glints of colour, sunlight.

Stir of echoes as the
Engine roars, drowning.
Through and through our
Last hope. To save the world
From its abominable doom.

If I live to see tomorrow,
My blessing will be counted.

We leave the atmosphere,
Burning, we have made it,
Earth is safe.

Matthew Hurst (11)
The Warwick School

CHINESE ZODIAC

Twelve chosen animals, one represents each year
There are also five elements to go with them I hear
Is there any truth in them?
Most people will deny.
It's amazing when you think about
Those animals in the sky.

A rat . . . an ox . . . a tiger . . . a ram
Hiding in the stars like a needle in sand.
A rabbit . . . a pig . . . a monkey . . . a snake
One hundred million years, to reach them it would take.
A dragon . . . a horse . . . a rooster . . . a dog
They're so hard to find, like searching in a fog.

Dancing in the sky with illuminated light
Living in the air with the darkness of night,
The twelve gifted animals chosen for their strengths
To prove themselves the greatest ones, they'll go to any lengths.

Martin Matthews (11)
The Warwick School

STAR SIGNS

Star signs are a way of life
They tell us what the future holds
We each have one which is our guide
To help us see what might unfold.

Mine is Virgo from September,
Hers is Scorpio from November.
Each has a sign to help us see
Which is the one for me!

Star signs are a way of life
They tell us what the future holds.
We each have one which is our guide
To help us see what might unfold.

Kayleigh-Jade Telfer (12)
The Warwick School

ZODIAC

There are twelve signs of the zodiac
One of them Leo
Leo the lion
His ruler is the Sun.
Leo's are protective, generous
And love to have fun.

There are twelve signs of the zodiac
One of them Cancer
Cancer the crab
His ruler is the Moon.
Cancerians are artistic, caring
Whose birthdays can be in June.

There are twelve signs of the zodiac
One of them Pisces
Pisces the fish
His ruler is Neptune.
Pisceans are emotional, creative
And up before noon.

Samantha Harding (11)
The Warwick School

SNAKES

A snake is a very slithery creature,
A-slipping and a-sliding are its best features.

There are adders, pythons and cobras too,
And snakes which can eat you, in one gulp or two.

There are venomous snakes, that kill you straight away,
And some snakes that kill, by suffocating their prey.

But there are some harmless snakes, which wouldn't hurt a fly,
And would rather make peace than cause you to die.

But either way, be careful or a snake may
Decide to make you its dinner today.

Ben Makroum (11)
The Warwick School

ZODIAC!

L   ibra is my star sign, it represents my birth date
     and I think it's really great!
I   ntelligent and bubbly, I try my best at everything
     it doesn't matter what!
B   eing there for everyone, friends and who I love,
     caring, sharing all good times, especially having fun!
R   eading and maths are such a bore, although I keep a balanced view
     I'd rather do my household chores!
A   lthough I'm sometimes very sad, my mum says I can be quite bad,
     and most of the time, I'm completely mad!

Charlotte Webb (12)
The Warwick School

I HAVE A DREAM

In the pouring rain,
In the pelting snow,
I dream a dream,
Such a wonderful dream,
A dream of spring,
And what fortune will bring for me,
I dream when everything appears to grow,
Butterflies and buzzing bees,
Fly around the sycamore trees,
The fluttering birds fly overhead,
As I wake up to the dawning chorus in my bed.

Brianne Marsden (11)
The Warwick School

ZODIAC

As I lie in bed, looking at the star-struck sky,
I think about star signs and what they are,
My star sign is Libra, am I like scales?
The glittery sky looks at me, collecting me in a daze.
Does the sky need my thoughts?
Does the world need my thoughts?
Am I in an endless train of thoughts?
Leading myself to an answer, not about Zodiac.
What is Zodiac, do I know?
Maybe my star sign is a mystery,
Please tell me stars, give me an answer.

Iain Powell (12)
The Warwick School

BUT WHAT ABOUT YOU?

I am a Libra,
Allowed to fly free.
But what about you?
Enough about me.

I am a Libra,
Gentle and kind.
But what about you?
What might you find?

I am a Libra
Romantic and fair,
But what about you?
You might be quite rare!

Rickey Bourne (12)
The Warwick School

FIREWORKS

*F*izz, crackle, pop go the fireworks;
*I*nto the sky with an enormous bang;
*R*eleasing their sparkling jewels into the Prussian-blue night;
*E*xplosions resounding off the nearby houses;
*W*onder is in the eyes of all, as the glittering sparks fall towards
                                        the uplifted faces;
*O*verhead is the beautiful pattern of multicoloured flecks;
*R*otating at an astonishing pace, the Catherine wheel spins;
*K*aleidoscopic colours, bright and electric begin to fade;
*S*igh, a massive sigh, as the pyrotechnics draw to a close.

Luke Dickerson (12)
Whitgift School

HARE'S BREADTH

The burning moon shudders brightly as
I skip through the daisies.
I am alone, free to contemplate
My struggle for survival.

A centrifuge of colours appear from side to side,
I scamper through knotted grass.
The earth slides unwittingly from beneath me,
I squint my ears, and yes.

Ear-shatteringly quiet, but yes,
My heart sobs as he stalks me,
His piercing smell shatters my nose,
His scalding shadow denting belief.

I spring and stutter to avoid that cold, red gaze,
But still he stalks me, allotting my death.
I mean no harm; I don't seek slaughter.
I sense his intent.

My ears hang desolately, painfully,
Yet I shall never surrender.
I approach the towering trees with caution,
And proceed, towering on stilts.

I feel no strength; maybe he'll tire,
We approach the rising, crimson sun in unison,
Through the haze I see it,
He lurches and lunges, and has me.

Then dark, again.

Ross Netherway (15)
Whitgift School

REDISCOVERING MY BODY

It had been so long since I had blown bubbles with my mouth.
Soft, hollow jellyfish I played with; each one
My childhood pet in a tank.

So long since, when hiccuping
I had poured fizzy drinks in regardless,
Catching a gassy waterwheel;
My diaphragm spluttering its disapproval
as I twiddled my clean thumbs.

And so long since I had seen the skin
covered for a year by rat-thick facial hair.
Now cut back; reluctant, pale,
Trying to cover its modesty with straggly vines.
I wash, and the pores gasp.

The apple juice is gone.
And I'm alone.

Martin Brown (18)
Whitgift School

MY ROUNDEL

When there are no more words and sounds
The time is stopping just for breathing,
The wind is blowing just for living,
The colours are creating rounds.

The people talk and still say nothing,
In churches they are counting pounds;
When there are no more words and sounds
The time is stopping just for laughing.

And there are no more sins that starving
Will look for food new brains and grounds,
There are no clouds, no rains, no mounds,
No newer meaning for the 'something'

When there are no more words and sounds.

Ion Martea (18)
Whitgift School

RELAXED, NOT SLOW

I crawl cautiously out, down the plank,
The dampness and rot slow me down.
Steadily, but hastily I reach the bottom,
Onto the warm, moist ground.

My trail sparkles, glistening in the sunlight,
It gleams across the dew-covered meadow.
A sigh of relief, no predators flying,
A fresh breeze drifts across my shell.

I haven't eaten since sunset,
Those leaves soaked in cool rainwater.
The path beyond me is clear and firm,
I try to avoid the boots of man.

I see a sparrow, it focuses on me,
I slither with pace beneath the trunk's shadow.
The bird gives up - it spots a cat,
I reveal myself and continue on.

I continue my travels, to find the others,
To seek greener pastures, find my food.
Whilst carrying my home upon my back,
Avoiding predators who follow my path.

Savio Moniz (15)
Whitgift School

KING AND COUNTRY

His hands are dimpled with age and war,
They twitch, muscles contracting desperately,
Trying to open a bar of chocolate.
Observed like an animal.
By the people he thought would never forsake him.

His hands are pale and corpse-like.
They are bare, no past, no present, no future,
Here is the last destination.
He has seen so much.
But no one seems to care.

His hands lead to an old shirt,
Blue and brown,
He fought for the freedom of others.
Not that it's important.
So did millions.

His hands have smothered with tense arms and a cloth.
His hands have gouged with desperate fingers at desperate eyes.
They have killed and maimed,
All for King and Country.
But they just patronise, a fairground attraction.

His hands lie by his side in the hospital morgue,
Hidden away,
Out of sight.
Out of mind.
Buried next to a rapist.

Alex Dawson (15)
Whitgift School

. . . Mmm

He sits hunched, staring glassily into space, tapping
resignedly on the scuffed wood of the table.
Waiting.
His fingers tap, trace
dance over the love lives of AR and TN
their hates, worries and exuberance
notched into the care-worn surface.
Waiting.
The clock on the
wall issues a
steady click
click, click
click to this counterpoint rhythm
under his fingers, his slumped
poise a testament to his powers of concentration.
Waiting.
The desk taunts him as his eyes move over its craggy
surface, his ears reverberating with
clichés, metaphors and adverbs,
head splitting
with infinitives
and puns.
Waiting.
His fingers flex irritably, pulsating in their Mexican
waves. Waiting.
Waiting.

He smiles.

Ben Winstanley (15)
Whitgift School

THE FISH

The silvery sardines slid through the sea
They moved as one body although they were many,
As a tight mass they squirmed through the water looking for food,
When they come to a rock they engulf it and reject it as they move on.
They move at great speeds in perfect unison and grace
Streaming through the sea throwing up a cloud of bubbles,
Illuminated by the sun peering down, the bubbles hide the swarm.
From the darkness of the deep a shadow flies,
A whale hurls itself through the icy water,
It opens its cavernous mouth and rushes at the innocent fish
                                                    from behind,
As if they had eyes in their tails, they turned swiftly and sharply away,
It worked, the whale plunged into the black, but surely it would be
back.
It came again and in the fish's flight it plucked a mouthful out,
Again and again the whale ploughed into the fish and caught a few,
Finally the barnacled monster left the swarm which now was
                                                    only one fish.
It wriggled away in an untidy manner, where had gone the grace?
The glassy sea was once again left in a deafening silence.

Sebastian Wood (14)
Whitgift School

THE ZODIAC

Scorpio scuttling through the sky,
He looks down on us like little ants.
Quickly he dodges between Leo and Aries,
Overlooking us with his menacing sting.

His beady eyes scanning for prey,
He sees a star shooting by,
Suddenly it is caught within his claws,
Scorpio standing strong in the misty sky,
His stars twinkling brightly.

Soon morning appears,
Scorpio is nowhere to be seen,
But tonight he'll come out,
Shining with pride and courage.

Daniel Lou (11)
Whitgift School

TREACLE

Inside of an oil painting,
Hidden forever from human eyes
Is a room. Floor to ceiling windows,
Grand piano, fruit bowl, wine rack,
And her. Tall, the way you think of a pencil,
And dark. Deliciously wrapped,
With dark hair, and dark eyes.
She glides across the floor,
And you wonder if her legs are moving
beneath that dark, pencil dress.
You get a throbbing feeling in your chest
Like you know you'll never be alone again,
Then you realise it's just her fingernails.
So suddenly her kisses turn to pain.
She pulls back, you see the
Thick, dark liquid on her lips.
Dark like oil, you hold her face,
And feel that darkness
Like treacle down your throat.
And you know that this will be
The last thing you ever do,
And you know that she will always be
Right here with you,
And her dress crumples onto the floor.

James Daly (15)
Whitgift School

ZODIAC

Not until your intelligent ruler Mercury confronts the Sun,
Will you fully be able to handle your finances with ease,
Given the lively cosmic activity currently affecting the
Money angle of your solar chart.
What that means to you or me is far beyond what I can think.

Can I really choose my future or is it set in stone,
Is this attempt to be a star just a protection from my fate?
With little thinking time bad mistakes are made,
Ones that I will regret at my journey's end.
And as I make a positive step, I'm halted by that fate.

Scorpios have good luck and fortune in their love
That's what they said last week and the week before.
But still there is no reward for all this work and strength,
And if I've been lucky in love I'm already dreading my downfall,
With bittersweet thoughts of romantic conclusions.

Would you really like to know the future?
Knowing what would happen at every twist and turn,
Shielding yourself from the smallest of problems,
As you already know that you can't overcome them.
What kind of life would I lead if I knew what to do without thinking?

We all say that we don't believe them 'just a guess or chance',
But whenever we can, we have a look,
Just to see if they've got anything good to say.
And we read, still intrigued trying to find lines of things,
That could happen to us in the coming day or week.

My destiny's not chosen yet,
But horoscopes make me forget,
My life is how I choose it to be,
No astrologist can write it for me.

Duncan Watson-Steward (15)
Whitgift School

DEATH

Death is but the end,
It is a common denominator in everyday life.
When you learn the truth about death
There is still a part of you that believes that death is but an eternal
sleep.

But the other half thinks about the blood-curdling trauma of death
and the dark hooded figure complete with scythe.

Yet, death cancels itself out in a way,
There is so much of it that we learn to respect it.
But then death is only around the corner,
It could be there when you go to work,
When you drink your first tonic in a bar,
Or when your neighbours mysteriously disappear.

It is like a spider;
Patient, but in the end it will always find a victim.
It waits silently in the middle of the system,
For any lost souls to fall into the trap for eternity.

It is an inevitable punishment for your sin,
It is irreversible,
Spontaneous,
The final showdown,
Your last living breath you take,
Your last struggle to make it through,
You build up your foundation
Just to come back crashing down on it,
And when you realize that existence is futile
You think . . . you think . . . you think . . .
And then black . . .

Edward Ash (13)
Whitgift School

CITY STORM

Towering buildings are blackened by the mind-controlling clouds,
And the neck-breaking gales engulf the night.
A sharp glimmer of blue falls from its fort,
And attacks its defenceless prey in its home.

Liquid acid falls from the enraged clouds,
Burning its cars to balls of intense heat,
While blistered buildings burn under blazing fires,
And the flying wall destroys all in its path.

The malevolent tempest expands out, covering eternity,
Looking to sate its hunger on the desolate streets.
Tapping on the pulsating panes of each house,
Howling like the unwelcome shadows of the dead.

We stand together, eagerly awaiting its riddance.
Hearing it crawling under the debilitated sandbags.
Hearing it scratching through the quaking trenches
As each desperately battle for their own survival.

Still the beast makes mortals tremble,
Seas of lions soar through the air,
Absorbing the sun's power and beauty,
And growing like an uncontrollable fire.

The marble drops descend.
Suffering structures drown
And all we can do is -
- wait.

Ben McFadden (15)
Whitgift School

THE ZODIAC

Virgo, the virgin, we are in debt of you;
When other gods turned their backs, you remained true.
Libra, the scales, the almighty judge,
Our good and bad deeds will make your scales budge.
Leo, the lion, king of all beasts,
Hercules' strong hands, made you deceased.
Aries, the golden ram, with horns hardest bone,
Jason used you to claim his rightful throne.
Taurus, the bull, in body but Zeus in mind,
Who wooed fair Europa with his gentle and kind.
Gemini, the twins, the greatest of friends,
Forever in the stars, together they will spend.
Cancer, the crab, sent down by Hera,
But Hercules killed you, and with you the Hydra.
Scorpio, the scorpion, who fought brave Orion,
But by your fatal poison, he died trying.
Sagittarius the archer, master of the bow,
Sagittarius, the teacher, all does he know
Capricorn, the goat, with fish's tail,
You are a son of Neptune, and love to sail.
Aquarius, the water bearer, captured by Zeus,
You fill the god's goblets with sweet nectar's juice.
Pisces, the fishes, great for a ride on,
You helped Aphrodite escape from the Typhon.
The zodiac, the constellations, you all are the best,
You all watch over us, from birth to death.

Tom Bond (13)
Whitgift School

TYNE COT CEMETERY, PASSCHENDAELE (MEMORIAL OF THE THIRD BATTLE OF YPRES, JUNE-NOVEMBER 1917)

A bright day, a clear blue bowl of sky.
Pure white stone and trimmed green grass.
The ranks on ranks of pure white stones.
Here is where I am happy.

Pure white, this silent mausoleum
for victims of this long-dead war.
And among the mute accusing stones
here I find my peace.

I walk amongst these dead
forgotten souls.
They walked in line to find their doom.
With them I feel at ease.

If I had but been born in time
to find this place in its first youth.
If I could find some meaning here
among these too, too many stones.

And outside of this place
I'm cold and I'm alone
I'm fighting in the concrete trenches under neon barbed wire.
Mortared by marketing and machine-gunned by images of Marilyn

But in here
between the silent, white rows
below the endless, open Flanders sky.
Here I can escape.

Alex Forbes (15)
Whitgift School

RECIPE FOR A VERY ANGRY FATHER

Take one sleeping father,
First shout until thoroughly stirred,
Then finely shred his paperwork,
Which should rattle some nerves.
Take all of his 'Des O'Connor' records,
And mix in with 'Daft Punk',
To get the mixture steaming.

Sprinkle many insults on the father,
Crush any remaining spirits,
Now the father should be sizzling,
Whisk speedily to his office,
Grill strongly,
Until your father cracks under your pressure,
And the truth slips out.

Put all the truth into one big bowl,
And save for later,
When the boss comes over.
Meanwhile the father should be almost done,
Whisk back to kitchen,
Drain all the beer,
Till smoke is simmering from him,
This tells you his anger is about to reach boiling point,
Hide under table,
Until everything boils over.

Tip: This could take many years.
Andrew McGrath has successfully performed this recipe.

Andrew McGrath (13)
Whitgift School

HUNTER HUNTED

Sleeping, watching, waiting,
What's the difference soon they will all be mine,
After all they are in my kingdom,
Under my watch.

Look at them,
Ignorant, miserable lives they lead,
Why I let them live,
I do not know.

What's that noise, could it be?
Yes, my meal is approaching me,
Unaware of my presence,
Unaware of its fate.

From the tall grass I pounced upon my foe,
It tries to run but I bat it with my huge paw,
Digging my claws in deep,
Still struggling, I bit its leg immobilising it.

I take the final bite,
Killing it.
I indulge myself in my prize kill,
I can now feast for days.

I hear another noise,
I look around, I see nothing,
I fear to investigate,
For I may lose my meal to a fellow predator.

I go into shock,
I see blood everywhere, my blood,
I've been shot, I feel queasy,
I am the hunter, hunted.

Adil Malik (16)
Whitgift School

178

THE ZODIAC

The first sign is *Aries*, the sign of the ram,
Bossy and headstrong, their key words are 'I am'.

Next is *Taurus* the bull, with his luxuries and food,
A meal in a five-star restaurant would put him in the mood.

Gemini is ruled by Mercury, the planet that's very hot,
These twins are said to be two-faced, and always talk a lot.

Cancer is the crab, who would never want to roam,
Always walking sideways, he loves his family and home.

I am *Leo* the lion, strong, wild and free,
Always king of the jungle - sounds a bit like me.

Virgo is the virgin, wearing a white dress,
Quiet, neat and tidy - nothing in a mess.

Libra is the one who wants to balance the scales,
Although he's undecided, justice never fails.

Scorpio is the scorpion, with the sting in his tail,
Don't get on the wrong side of him or he'll make you scream and wail.

Sporty *Sagittarius*, the archer, lucky with his bows,
Could hit the bullseye on Jupiter, any time he chose.

Capricorn the mountain goat, should never be a flop,
He's daring and ambitious, always reaching for the top.

Aquarius the water carrier is zany and mad,
Wearing brightly coloured clothes, he never seems sad.

Pisces are the fish, swimming in two different ways,
Sensitive and dreamy, as if in a daze.

Charlie Tuckey (11)
Whitgift School

THE EAGLE HAS LANDED

I am the most predatory, fantastic, living thing,
I sit on top of my domain, watching my subjects below me.
Of the forest, I am the high ruler, they call me the forest King,
I will start my hunting voyage now; from my nest I flee.

The crystal, wrinkly sea beneath me crawls,
As I soar high above.
I watch my prey, far away, from the mountain walls,
I will catch my prey inside my crooked glove.

My eyesight is impeccable, I close in on prey below,
I leave the cliffs and hurtle towards it at a supersonic speed;
Now it is time for my hunting skills, to get into their flow,
Down I swoop, *splash*. It is done, my infamous deed.

They all look upon me, jealous of what they see,
I ride the currents, high or low in the air
The way I soar, the way I am, full of grace and the way I be
Everyone wants to be the Eagle; life is not fair.

The greatest wingspan I have been granted,
With my wings, in the daylight sky, I glide and glide,
Down below, all the trees, named after me have been planted,
From the daylight sky, I soar through to the evening tide.

I fly back to my domain, with prey in hand,
I tear the fish with my cragged-hooked claws
The scraps get thrown to my subjects on the land
I am perfection, I the Eagle have no flaws.

I am God's gift to hunting, a hunting King,
Neither fish nor prey has ever got the better of me.
In the forest, I have control of every little thing,
From the foxes to the birds, from the ants to the bees.

I must now have my rest,
The eagle, king of kings, is the best.

Anuj Mohindra (14)
Whitgift School

THE STREETS

The hustle!
The bustle!
In the streets the people
Excited, happy, bored, sad
Listening to the cries of the market staller
Worrying inside
Supporting his family is harder than he thought

The rich businessman stares out of his first floor window
Feeling little pity for the man wrapped in newspaper
lying on the park bench
Or the old lady being lifted into the ambulance
But why should he?
None of this affects him

So that's OK then . . .
Isn't it?

William Hall (13)
Whitgift School

Journey Through The Milky Way

Only people from that star sign will
experience the full joys.

Those in Aries shall open their eyes,
To a hillside with a stream running through,
A goat grazing on bright green grass,
They shall fall back to sleep as the sun goes down.

The people of Taurus shall wake in Spain,
In a bullring in front of hundreds,
They watch as the bull prepares to charge,
As he charges their eyes will close.

The Gemini shall see a second roller coaster,
On which the ride is opposite to calm and relaxing,
The other will look tatty and you will see your twin,
They will fall asleep thinking twice the amount.

Those of Leo shall be on the African plains,
They will see a lion pounce at them,
Not land on them, but instead the antelope next to them,
And go back to sleep seeing the full beauty of the lion's mane.

The people in Sagittarius will wake in the forest,
They will hear galloping and see a half-man, half-horse appear,
He will be hunting with his bow and arrow,
They shall sleep again as an arrow rips through the air.

Oliver Stoten (11)
Whitgift School

THE ZODIAC

On the night train, as the windows rattle,
I gaze out on the starlight battle.
Of darkness enveloping light,
A horribly destructive fight,
Of chaos evil, dark and dreary,
And constellations different and cheery.
There's Taurus, the mighty bull,
And Scorpio and more dangerous still,
Pisces, the submarine spy,
All using cunning, danger and sly,
Methods of surviving through without doubt,
A horribly destructive bout.
And this grudge must be evenly matched,
Because forever these stars are the same batch!
On the night train, as the windows rattle,
I gaze out on the starlight battle.

David Ralf (12)
Whitgift School

THE SQUIRREL

Perched upon the crimson-red fence
Eyes darting from place to place
Fluffy, red tail raised behind it
Its eyes catch a brown chestnut on the ground
And without a second thought it leaps into the air
It skims through the air without waking a single soul
Diving as if the hard concrete floor was a soft, deep pool of water
Its small paws hit the ground first with a small tap
And then the rest of the body follows
It grabs the nut with both paws and starts to nibble.

Adeeb Hossain (13)
Whitgift School

THE ANTARCTIC

No life lives here except its natives:
A seal or polar bear.
This is because, the deadly cold, is a disease,
Spreading with ease,
Stripping its victims bare.

This intense cold has claimed many innocent lives,
And as it struck them,
They soon knew that their death was soon,
Because it hit them like a thousand knives.

Thus, no one knows what secrets lie beneath,
Where mystery prevails,
But even if they did, which I very much doubt,
They don't live to tell the tale.

So outsiders be warned!
Never go where conditions are grim,
Because I'll tell you now, and be assured,
You'll be knocking on the gates to heaven.

Chris Hurst (13)
Whitgift School

THE STARS

Our stars, praised as the angels since the dawn of time,
The light of many as they shine,
They come upon us from the heavens,
As they twinkle they burn with fierce passion,
The candles of night.

They come down on us as guardians of the sky,
Protecting us as we sleep in our beds,
The magical celestial bodies in constellations,
They shine, inspire and fascinate many,
A piece of nature's art.

As we gaze into the sky, their warm glow makes us calm,
A guide to those who walk the night away,
At one with the wilderness
And a final resting place of the honourably departed.

Dan Ho (13)
Whitgift School

I'D LIKE TO BE A MUSHROOM

I'd like to be a mushroom,
And lie around all day;
Soaking up the sun,
In a mushroom kind of way.

I crave to be a mushroom,
A toadstool one maybe,
And sit around the garden,
And have a cup of tea.

I wouldn't have to do a thing,
Not one thing in my life,
I wouldn't have to do exams;
Avoiding all the strife.

Oh, let me be a mushroom,
Please, please, please, please, please
I'll brush my teeth every night,
And live on a diet of cheese.

Being a mushroom would be bliss,
I want to be one now,
There's just one disadvantage,
Getting eaten by a cow.

Jamal Sondhi (13)
Whitgift School

SCORPIO

The immortal Scorpio
is the sign to which I belong
My back arched, my claws ready
I always have a sting in my tail.

My kingdom is one of power
I want to dominate all
My talents are used
For my well being.

My pride is as strong
As my desire
I am masterful and deep
My secrets are kept to myself.

My strongest emotion is jealousy
I have two different faces
I can succeed where others fail
For in my eyes, I am the best.

I use my charm and wit
To get me where I want
I love success and glory
I always bide my time.

I know the dark side of life
I know my inner feelings
I could move Heaven or Hell
With one single look.

I can be vengeful
I can be kind
Whatever feelings I have
I make them known.

Soon all people will know
I am a Scorpio.

Sam Kerr (13)
Whitgift School

MY STAR SIGN

As I gazed into the stars one night,
I wondered,
Would I be gentle,
Would I be strong,
Would I be anything like my star sign,
As I gazed into the stars?
I found what I was looking for,
My star is Taurus,
Taurus the bull.
Taurus, Taurus, that was his name,
With the speed of a cheetah,
And the strength of an elephant,
I wondered, just wondered,
Would I be anything,
Just like him.

Mihir Desai (13)
Whitgift School

STAR SIGN OF THE ZODIAC

Silly as it may be, this is only one way of telling the future,
Tarot cards can also reveal someone's life.
As the magazine goes round the office the workers gather round,
Ridiculously trying to see what will happen tomorrow.

Sighs of joy or disappointment as the next day finally comes,
Incredibly a prediction has come true.
Great pain of jealousy comes from those who haven't got that fortune,
Never mind, it can come true next week.

Only twelve star signs,
For over twenty million people.

Taurus, Pisces, the charming Libra,
Have one thing all in common,
Extraordinary beliefs that what they read is true.

Zoology of the sky is common,
Observatories of the ancients found them.
Defining stars and people by patterns,
Immediately describing their characters.
Accurately or not, as the case may be,
Catching the poor punters out.

Andrew Robertson (14)
Whitgift School

THE LAMENT OF THE TREE

I fear the wrath of the Lord of the Night
I fear the power of his storm
I have no comrades for help or to home
The animals have all gone.

I am stripped of my jade armour, my soul and friends
I shoulder the burden of dare
Silence stares back at my passionate laments
Nobody seems to care.

The night draws near, his winds increase
I feel myself now going numb
As light withers and dies all life seems to cease
For judgement day has come.

Sean Noronha (13)
Whitgift School

ZODIAC

I hear Rembrandt drew self-portraits,
From his image in the mirror.

So I look into my mirror of stars, into another universe.

The boy in my mirror peers back at me.
He wears a pleasurable, jolly smile, a pair of glasses
And has short hair with his fringe up.

Behind him in the corner a shining silver flute on a metal music stand,
A computer with a waterfall of CD cases,
A desk with paper like all the feathers moulting from a bird,
A huge bed with armies of soft toys ready for action,
Lego and K'nex designed for carpet racing.
A leaning tower of books like Pisa on his sofa,
And a bookshelf packed so tight it could be a brick wall.
Posters of the planets and the ram riding high.
Bats and balls in boxes, judogi thrown down: ippon!
A box transmitting images onto the screen,
A hole in the wall with a glaring fire reaching out of it.
Games boxes stacked high like skyscrapers.

This is his zodiac; his twelve constellations.

Ben Cook (11)
Whitgift School

MUDDLED?

In the snowy drifts, flittering gatheringly at the North Pole,
The snow kangaroos slither sinuously around,
The white water coral stampedes in a fasteous manner,
And the ice worms nibble mumbiously through the blocks.

On the coral reefs, hanging around the warm seas,
Large antelope swim flumsily,
Golden chairs flutter flimsily on the hot icicles,
And polar bears fluffily wallow in the shallows.

On the moon, flying gracefully round the sun,
Cows munch grazingly at the lush pastures,
Sharks plod around ponderously at minute intervals,
And frocks frolic around happily over the musty craters.

In our largish magnificentness of schoolish buildings,
Army troops trundle around marchingly,
Scientists gargle talkingly over large spooktacles,
And babies gargle at garish dogs.

On the tippy toppy of tedious trees,
Donkeys doodle dangerously at heights
Hippos flu foolishly, frilling around slots,
And flumps flutter frumpishly, flooping floppy flicle froggies.

Ni happy frolic schooltide nee-ing warble
Scattering ni scottles of parlous cootiously
Ddfsk, aleaa ituah Ifaka finn.

Christian Brown (13)
Whitgift School

THE GREAT WAR

The Great War was a terrible thing
Men at war with each other
Even we did not know why we were here
Risking our lives for an unknown reason.

The sound of gunfire breaks the silence
It scares the men senseless
All the officers enjoy banquets
While all we have is cold food.

The women at home urged their brave men on
Giving them feathers if they didn't
Go! They said Go! Make us proud
Attack these autocrats and come back soon.

But alas, many did not
Those who were brave enough, died in their thousands
From exploding shells or machine guns
Our heroes stayed in their muddy graves
Never to be found again.

Those who did come back safe
Were treated as heroes
But as we remember our dead
The vision of the cloudy skies
The muddy, rat-infested trenches
And the rotting bodies come back to me
Stronger than the year before.

Bravin Thillainathan (13)
Whitgift School

UNDERNEATH

Enter,
The large hall of pure black dust and grey smoke,
with computers churning out slim, pink permits.
Ladies and men in uniform, stare out of their claustrophobic
                                                          compartments
and out at the great dull hall with tired, weary, swollen eyes
                                        and cigarettes in their mouths.

Nearby other men and women in uniform chat and giggle but they
subtly keep a close eye to the bubbling tourists and shattered
                                                          commuters.
The separate gates accept the tickets and flicker opening and closing
in the space of a second.

Down the eternal escalator with a bewildering wind rustling your hair
from different directions, and the notorious *loud* crescendoing
humming, buzzing with an engine raring to go . . .

A floor is clear at the end of this eternal escalator with five different
passages taking you to five different platforms.
Onto the platform, with dark deranged tunnels taking you to the
forgotten and to the forbidden.

That hum and buzz is heard, unsure of which tunnel, yet suddenly
on the left a light appears with the hum getting louder and louder
and a light shines which gets brighter and brighter . . .

A grey worm appears, it stops gently, its doors open softly and
almost immediately people spill out and more fill in.
Doors shut, whistles blow, and it smoothly floats away with the
humming whispering all disappearing, silently away.

Myuran Palarajah (13)
Whitgift School

ZODIAC

Leo, the golden and the warm-hearted lion,
The brave and intolerant ruby of the zodiac.

Aquarius, the blue and friendly servant of Uranus,
The honest and loyal sapphire of the symbols.

Cancer, the silver and emotional crab,
The sensitive but sharp pearl of the moon.

Capricorn, the grey and sensible servant of Saturn.
The patient and careful jet of the zodiac.

Aries, the scarlet and the adventurous ram.
The courageous and enthusiastic diamond of Mars.

Gemini, the yellow and intellectual servant of Mercury.
The youthful and lively crystal of the signs.

Libra, the pink and stylish scale.
The romantic and charming servant of Venus.

Pisces, the violet and compassionate servant of Neptune.
The noble yet secretive amethyst of the zodiac.

Sagittarius, the brown and cheerful archer.
The concerned and helpful servant of Jupiter.

Scorpio, the black and determined scorpion.
The powerful and passionate topaz of the symbols.

Taurus, the cream possessive bull.
The patient and reliable servant of Venus.

Virgo, the white and shy virgin.
The practical and diligent jasper of the signs.

Hemal Thaker (11)
Whitgift School

BETTER TO DIE?

To live
How to live like filth,
Like creatures of the mud.
Simply parasites of society.
How to live?

To live
How to live with death,
It creeps silently, looking.
Feeding time soon.
How to live?

To live
How to live with life,
Foul crawling life.
Born to die.
How to live?

To live
How to live neglected,
Stench of alcohol.
He's back.
How to live?

To live
How to live without hope,
False hopes crafted.
Safety in sleep.
How to live?

How to live like this?
Who?
Who indeed?

Mike McEwan (14)
Whitgift School

DIVING OFF GURTEEN PIER

'Twas a tempestuous day.
The cormorants circled overhead
As if taunting me.
From the safety of the pier
I stared into the murky black depths
Of the cold Atlantic.
The sinister mountains loomed.
The slatey, leaden, irascible sky
Seemed to compress me like a roof.
The sinuous weeds
Looked so far beneath me.
'Come on! Come on!'
Shrieked the cousins.
'It's lovely! It's so warm!'
As they bobbed and splashed about.
Petrified, I clenched my fists.
My heart thumped.
I shut my eyes,
And jumped.
Before I knew anything
Kerplush!
Everything was green.
I came to the top, gasping for air.
The sun seemed to beam down
As if to congratulate me.
I got out straightaway
And walked up the steps
Feeling a hero.

Richard Rose (11)
Whitgift School

THE WHALE

The wind howls
The waves break
Something moves
A whale wakes.

From the uncharted depths
Rises the giant of the sea
More powerful than any
And too quick to see.

He dives back down
And jumps up so high
Three fish in his mouth
But still as hungry as ever, is he.

The birds watch craning their necks
Just able to see
The giant of the ocean
Oh, so splendid to see.

How cold it must be
To live under the sea
No warmth in the ocean
Just like ice-cold tea.

Tim Postlethwaite (13)
Whitgift School

BUTTERFLY FLUTTERBY

Butterflies entrance
Around the garden they prance
In a colourful dance

Patterns so beautiful
With two wings so powerful
They are successful.

High up they flutter
In the bright sun they glitter
Past trees they skitter.

They fly up so high
Into the dazzling sky
I wish I could fly.

Krish Ambalawaner (14)
Whitgift School

THE MATCH

The boys charged out upon the field
Determined that we'd never yield

The rugby match was set to start
The team was armoured with stout heart

The whistle blew, a cheer was raised
Feet thundered by, no one was fazed

The ball was passed with glorious ease
Tackles were made like felling trees

Points were scored, our feelings high
All players senses, a win was nigh

Then, oh disaster, a catastrophic pass
A try for *them*, it must be the last!

The kick was good and all was tied
A murmur rippled through our side

The ball was loose, our captain dived
He crossed, we kicked, we had survived.

Yosuke Saraoka (14)
Whitgift School

THE ZODIAC

As I look up into the sky,
I see it,
I see the great and mighty lion, Leo.
As he stars down at us like little blades of grass,
We hear his thunderous roar and gaze at his ferocious mouth.
I then take a closer look and realise that Leo
Is not such a meat-eating monster,
But a soft, gentle creature
With feelings and a heart of understanding.
Like an oyster,
It looks hard and unbreakable,
But on the inside a whole new creature,
Soft and venerable, gentle and kind.

Christopher Lawlor (11)
Whitgift School

THE OAK

He stands
Firmly anchored into the ground
Like an ancient monument from the beginning of time
Protecting the innocent horse chestnuts
Guarding them from the elements
Withstanding the test of time
As guard and protector
Like a high and mighty judge
Showing his authority
And directing the skyline
With his gigantic brothers
Over the great, green forest.

Marcus Pieters (13)
Whitgift School

THE WAR

The panic of the war sweeps through my head,
Red mud soaks through my old and tattered boots,
As I run through the heap of bloodstained dead,
I joined the war to kill the 'Nazi-brutes',
But now my heart cries for what I have done
And now I don't care, I just want to live.
To see my land freed from the 'evil Hun',
I wish, I wish, I still had more to give,
Alas, but now I see myself slowing,
A dead man walking, no tears left to cry.
I say my last prayer. My eyes glowing,
I cannot help but think I am to die
My sad heart completely emptied of hope,
I feel myself falling, I cannot cope.

Jack Offord (13)
Whitgift School

ZODIAC POEM

Z   ooming through the skies at the speed of light
O   rbiting exquisite sights
D   iscovering unknown yet bewitching
I   liuminating constellations to show various star signs like
A   quarius the water bearer, Leo the lion
C   ancer the crab, Virgo the virgin

P   isces the fish, Libra the balance
O   scillating in and out of constellations
E   nchanting yet mysterious scenes
M   any more mysteries revealed on this unique voyage.

Rakin Anwar (11)
Whitgift School

London . . . A Dream For Many

London is a city of gold
Everything is stereotypically made of riches
The streets
The lamps
The houses
Everything.

We, however, have not accounted for its intellectuality
For it draws us to it
Speaking of wonders beyond our wildest dreams
London, however, is a cruel schizophrenic
It is dark, putrid and foul
We think it is sweet, light and fair
But it is not.
London is not weak but dominant
Any person who is weak and poor should not challenge London
They will perish if they do.
Stay away from this barbaric city
London is more lethal than the Romans
Far more observant than Sherlock Holmes
More calculating than Archimedes!

Ali Khan (12)
Whitgift School

The Zodiac

Horoscopes are there to be doubted
I am sure that you all will agree,
That the facts written in magazines
Must be wrong in some degree.

I am a Virgo, and I must say
That I don't fit the characteristics they give
But surely the moon and the stars cannot tell
The way that our lives will be lived!

Horoscopes are there to be doubted,
I am sure now you all will agree
That the people who write this are always wrong
Or the whole world is strange, except me.

Ifor Capel (12)
Whitgift School

NIGHT

Troubled slumber, fitful waking,
Echoing softly through night air.
Cauldrons of fear eternally cooking
The dream ends, the nightmare begins.
Clouds of sorrow reflected in demons' eyes
The world in the sheath of a dagger.

Ancient temples, ruins and darkness,
The fires of stories fanned by rumours.
Creatures sleep warily, hiding from
Make-believe spectres, spirits and such,
Superstition and blasphemy.

The sky burns red,
Clouds break,
Hope shines.

The new sun's light pours from high clouds,
Fresh dawn smells lingering,
Birds flocking from land to sea
Under the cage of the sky.
The air alive like a newborn child,
The terrible terrors gone from the earth,
Ever changing.

James Gin (12)
Whitgift School

ZODIAC

Zodiac, the space roller coaster, wants to take you on a ride,
A ride through the galaxy, where you'll meet all the stars,
Where you'll find all twelve star signs,
And within ten minutes of zooming through the cosmic sky,
You'll be back home on Earth.

It wants you to step on board for the journey of your life,
A journey you'll never forget,
Whizzing through the stars and planets,
Racing meteorites as you go thundering past,
Wishing it could go on forever and ever.

Rocking left and right,
Rapidly cruising towards the sun,
Spinning swiftly past the galaxies,
As fast as space rockets,
Discovering brand new planets.

The amazing zodiac will travel through thick and thin,
So fasten your seatbelts and get ready to rumble,
It wants to take you for a spin!

Farhaz Jammohamed (12)
Whitgift School

MYTHS AND LEGENDS

It sits there silent, yet telling all
Containing villains, heroes at a ball.
It holds life not yet found
But within their pages they are bound.

Stories told of damsels encaged,
New visions with each passing page
Giants, Magi, jumping cows
Or pea-green boats with flaring bows.

Within its printed pages lie
A realm where nothing shall ever die,
A land of hopes and dreams
Where nothing can go wrong, or so it seems!

Legends, myths, quests of old
Racing for the unclaimed gold
For the ultimate prize of being told!

Jason Tun (13)
Whitgift School

THE ZODIAC

Stars, fate, life, death,
What do people call a *zodiac?*
You decide, you pick, you answer it.

Aries, Taurus, Gemini, Cancer, Leo, Virgo, Libra, Scorpio, Sagittarius,
Capricorn, Aquarius, Pisces,
Just a pot of baloney or true, life helping fate.

Mercury sizzling, Venus destructive, Earth breathing, Mars iced,
Jupiter liquidated, Saturn ringed,
Uranus 21-year days, Neptune 165-year year,
Pluto freezing.

Living, dying, what more important
Than these two events?
Take back your buying and selling, take back your taking and giving.

Do the stars rule our life? Or planets?
Or do we?
Answer that and you shall be one step closer to the meaning of life.

Sam Oughton (11)
Whitgift School

THE ZODIAC

The zodiac appears very rarely,
It is a feared creature, but nobody
Knows exactly what it looks like.
People reckon it comes out of a
Devilish hell in the darkest corner of the universe.

People have thought to see him,
But his identity stays a mystery.
Those who dare seek him never return.
So people have stopped their search.
Those who survived dare not speak but one.

He tells us of a beast, horrible
With teeth the size of a sword's blade.
He wears a mask, but you can see the
Red of his eyes.

This vile creature still lives,
The zodiac is the best way to describe him, and the safest.

Theo Whyte (11)
Whitgift School

WHY OH WHY?

Why oh why, did the war have to start?
Who could have done such a thing?
And anyone, who in this deed took part,
Has made many funeral bells ring.

Why oh why, did we have this tragedy?
So many lives have been lost.
Now all the world is never happy,
Huge buildings now reduced to dust.

How on earth, did one man do this?
He must be terribly evil,
And all this time, when people are mourning,
He is living safe on a hill.

Why oh why, did the war have to start,
Who could have done such a thing?
And anyone, who in this deed took part,
Has made many funeral bells ring.

Steven Jefferies (12)
Whitgift School

THE NIGHT

Darkness comes,
Comes every night,
Stars shooting,
Disappearing.
You're safe inside,
You have no fear,
Except for shadows,
That lurk too near.
Clouds wondering,
Staying silent,
How could anything,
Be so quiet.
Floorboards creaking,
People moving,
Radiators gurgling,
Foxes screeching.
But I'm at home,
Dreaming of sleeping.
Darkness comes,
Comes every night.

Edward Harrison (12)
Whitgift School

THE ZODIAC

Aquarius -
the provider of water, so sacred to life.
Pisces -
a feather in air, floating without making waves.
Aries -
the ram with the healing fleece, sacrificed for saving.
Taurus -
a never-ending power struggling to control itself.
Gemini -
the twins not to part for a second for loss of each other.
Cancer -
and its pincers bring fear, as its name does to people.
Leo -
is the most proud of animals and knows it too well.
Virgo -
the untouched beauty - love never coming her way.
Libra -
is so perfect, balanced on both sides with good and bad.
Scorpio -
is never to be crossed, its sting a deadly weapon to all.
Sagittarius -
the archer, a great aim to any unwary foe.
Capricorn -
the great escapee who was sacrificed for life.

Charlie Thomas (11)
Whitgift School

THE ZODIAC

Capricorn the goat starts off the year,
Through winter's hardship we persevere,
Aquarius of water is not too far behind,
Pouring his warm vessel on the frozen waters,
Pisces the fish swims through the now merry waters,
Listening as the sprites sing and dance at the side,
Aries the ram charges through the field,
Crashing through a bush and jumping a stream,
Taurus the bull charges doggedly on,
His tail and hair whipping in the wind,
Gemini the twin daughters of mercy,
March on to the next year,
Cancer the giant crab scuttles along the shore,
Looking for a tasty morsel washed up by the tide,
Leo the lion pounces with fluidity,
Bringing honour to those who touch him,
Virgo the maiden walks in all her glory,
Her grace a blessing to those who behold her,
Libra weighs the scales of day and night,
For at this time they are equal,
Scorpio the scorpion stings enemies to the ground,
While fighting off others with his claws,
Sagittarius gallops holding a bow,
A good shot and precise to the point.

Simon Hardy (11)
Whitgift School

THE SCORPION

Its dark plates of armour upon,
The repugnant, acid flesh within,
The deep cavity in his heart,
Of this beast with dark intent.

His heart is a cavity in his chest,
So deep and blackened,
With no feelings down in there,
He only feels irate and evil,
Wanting to kill . . . wanting to kill,
There is no one who can calm his rage.

His sting, how black and sharp it is,
With a venomous sac below,
The power of the force concealed within,
Can kill a full-grown man!
He controls it only by devilish impulse,
And it strikes, strikes, strikes, with force.

The claws are twisted, evil and thin,
As he sees his foe he strikes with the sting,
But his second weapon is his claws,
With which he crushes his fallen victim.
Those claws, have force so great,
That they can crush you in an instant.

Alexander Nesbitt (12)
Whitgift School

THE ZODIAC

There are many signs but one is special to me,
Aries, it may also be special to you,
For you and I may share the same feeling.
From the Aries constellation,
Zodiac.

This magical belt fills the skies,
As they sit like stepping-stones side by side,
Zodiac.

Watching stars and comets wandering by,
Looking at so many that you think maybe I will see it,
Zodiac.

Just thinking about them is still wonderful,
But one day I know I will see it,
Zodiac.

This imaginary belt up in the heavens,
Lies in our deep, black space,
Zodiac.

Along with the sun, moon and planets,
Are 12 different sets of stars which are called . . .
The zodiac.

John Mensah (11)
Whitgift School

THE ZODIAC

Looking in the night sky,
I see the zodiac from time to time.
The billions of stars around the sky,
Form patterns to show the sign.
There is Sagittarius,
Who is optimistic and honest,
But on the other side he is careless and irresponsible.
Sagittarius is known in the sky,
As a half man and half bull.
In fact there are eleven different symbols,
All with the same way to describe them.
Sadly they do not appear often,
But when you see it is a spectacular sight.
If you dare go on the zodiac ride,
You will see the different symbols of the zodiac.
On the walls of 'The Zodiac' there seems to be billions of stars,
And without realising it is a ride it feels like you are in space.
But beware the twists and turns,
It makes your stomach turn somersaults.
We ask ourselves,
How was the zodiac invented at such an early stage,
Where they did not have telescopes?
We all have many questions to ask,
But now we must enjoy the sight.

Ranjeet Sandhu (12)
Whitgift School

ICE

Ice is that feeling, when petrified of the immortal,
It is that vigorous and despicable evil that haunts the world.
Ice is that unpredictable misfortune that everybody experiences.
It is the white in the Union Jack irritably freezing the country.
Ice is what lies ahead of you when you have sinned.
It is a whimsical prison, capturing the good and freezing the bad.
Ice is that force, which is impressionable upon evil, which is
the force that values its existence.
It is a foe that brings sorrow to many.
Ice makes people suffer, and makes people hate.
It is a demon that surreptitiously forces you to do wrong.
Ice is a mass murderer, wanted by all, except for its followers,
who seek power and to be feared and want to have
all unimportant qualities.

Alex Romaines (12)
Whitgift School

SIGNS OF THE ZODIAC

G iving and generous are its attributes
E nergetic and lively spirits
M eek but strong is its character.
I nsecure, it never will be
N ever slow, but quick to realise
I ts energy never ceases to be otherwise.

Christopher Champion (13)
Whitgift School

THE CRICKET MATCH

We inspected the wicket which was really flat
We won the toss and elected to bat.
Our skipper had such dreadful luck
He was out first ball for a golden duck.
In I went at number three
Hoping to score a century.

The bowler delivered an easy wide
I struck the ball to the off side.
The crowd gave out a mighty roar
The ball rolled over the line for four.
My knees were knocking, I was in a fix
I slogged the ball up in the air for six.

On came the new bowler he looked a creep
I hit a four with a fine reverse sweep
The score crept up run by run
Up goes my bat I get a ton.
Our innings was over with a magnificent score
The oppo were chasing 250-4.

We were fired up as we came out to bowl
To bowl them out was our goal.
We appealed and gave a huge shout
Up went the finger the batsman was out.
The innings was over quickly I took a fine catch
To my delight I was voted Man of the Match.

Fred Woodrow (11)
Whitgift School

To The Stars

On my way to the stars I met the magician
He helped me so much; he planned to rule the world,
That reminded me of me a bit,
I had just set off to the stars.

If all was right, I had met the dwarf of time
The iron fist of nature,
I persuaded him that black was white
That was what I did.

The dwarf was pretty calm at first, he reminded me of a Libran
He talked himself out of my woe,
I *am* calm,
Elves were waiting for my coming.

He called me 'brave heart',
I took that as *a* compliment,
Gemini are the best he claimed
My brain started to twist

I was pushing myself to success,
The last ring he *said* was the ring of power
I knew what he was talking about,
The ring found its way; that's what I had to do.

His short temper drew him nearer to my name
'Elliott' he shouted!
Now I had to leave
That was the deal anyway.

Gemini had turned against me.

Elliott Chambers (11)
Whitgift School

THE DANCING BEAR

I walked through the bright fir trees.
I felt a rumble in the ground.
Curiosity flowed through my veins.
What was there?

I heard a screech echoing through the wood.
With the lovely melody from a violin.
The sounds were so strange.
What could it be?

When I pushed through the bushes to get a look
What a treat for the eyes was there.
A brown-coated bear with a dull old tramp.
What were they doing there?

The bear's beady eyes were bright with excitement
As he danced to the beat of the tune.
But his eyes filled with sadness when he scratched on the chain.
How could the tramp be so cruel?

The tramp turned around with black strange eyes
And shouted 'Is anyone there?
Please be a dear and give money to the blind.'
How could I ever refuse?

James McNeilly (11)
Whitgift School

THE ZODIAC

The zodiac
Flashes like
A star with
Beams of light
Spurting from behind
But the zodiac
Isn't a star
The zodiac
Is a long cylinder
Aliens are in it
It goes fast
Through space
The aliens are long
With three arms
Short
With no legs
They have no skin
Just a wobbly substance
They are the
Universe's greatest drivers
And they drive
The universe's
Greatest vehicle:
The zodiac.

Adam Jordan (11)
Whitgift School

THE STORM

There was silence.
The gloom deepened.
A brewing storm waited patiently among the fluent movement
of the swirling winds.
The ever-blackening sky gradually devoured the sun.
Oncoming waves met their fate on rocks lying on the beach.
Thundering, savage water attacked the dark, barren caves.
Lightning thrust through the thick, heavy clouds.
The silence was broken.
The ground gave way to my weight.
Squelching mud surrounded my feet.
I ran.

The road seemed to be endless.
Rain struck my already aching body.
Heavily breathing, heart pounding, trying to find someone.
Even though I knew; I was alone,
I was lost.
I stumble to my knees.
The intense exhaustion overwhelms me.
I hold on to my last breath.
This cruel, hostile world engulfs my presence.
I fall . . .
I fade.

Samy Rashad (14)
Wimbledon College

HONOUR/DISHONOUR?

What if man fought himself?
United only by their enemies
their purpose of conflict small, gathered for a better conflict.
Initial purpose, insignificant
what if man has no desire, no long for conflict?

We die for something small, it always is
We live for something great, it never will be
We work for a greater power,
What gives it power, what gives it superiority?

Why do we fight, because we differ
Why do we disagree, because we have fought
The great paradox creates more violence
As the ball of infinite difference escalates
The violence is flowing like a river, impossible to stop.

We are the voice of difference, unison brings discord
Assonance brings dissonance, synonym and antonym.
Being unique brings difference, being same brings friction.

No reason, yet they are provoked by each action.
The ideas of fair, honesty, leads to loss of life.
Who would keep dignity, when there is nothing left?
We have an honour, something beyond physical matter,
yet, the pride we wear as a medal, a sash.

We can see the honour that we wear,
we lose everything, risk all, just for the few words:
'Well done, congratulations, you are honour.'

Michael Pereira (15)
Wimbledon College

THE DOVE

The dove
As white as snow
As white as the clear clouds
As graceful and elegant as the swan
As quiet as a fish through water
Hovering higher
And higher still
As high as the trees
As high as the clouds
Swerving as accurately as a hawk
Detecting danger in a second
Panicking
No longer as elegant and graceful as the swan
Speeding away
Not knowing where to go
Tired but can't stop
But can't go on
The dove
The dove gives in to fate
Suddenly
Crush
The eagle makes a kill
The dove
No longer white
No longer elegant
No longer graceful;
But still quiet of course
The dove
The dove is no more.

Liam Healy (12)
Wimbledon College

THE TEDIOUS, TERRIFYING TEMPEST

A grey gloom settled over the sky,
The hairs on the back of my neck trembled,
My heart began to pound,
As the thing was collecting pace.

The silence boomed around me,
Then I heard a deafening howling,
That died away in its own echo,
Which sent a chill down my spine.

The brewing, howling tempest growing never weary,
Shrieked deafeningly,
As an aggressive, chilled, steel-like wind,
Swept my weather-beaten face.

The thundering, walloping waves
Were like rough cat's claws,
Reaching for its hopeless prey,
Stranded on the shore.

The heavens opened.
Rain pelted down
Like bullets,
Piercing the sand.

Here I am, exposed to the elements
So brutal,
Lethal,
Eerie.

Cormac van der Hoeven (14)
Wimbledon College

THE MYSTERY OF LIFE

Where are we going? Why are we here?
What's it all about? What is it we fear?
Is it a journey? Is it a game?
What does it mean, this thing with no name?

The day, the night, the wind, the rain,
Are we in anguish? Are we in pain?
Why are we cheerful? Why depressed?
This ancient mystery, left unaddressed.

What is the meaning of life, they all say?
What is the game of chance we all play?
Is it a notion? Is it a dream?
What is this life? What does it mean?

Niam Dodd (14)
Wimbledon College